Vocabulary and Spelling Book

McDougal Littell

GRADE SIX

McDougal Littell
A HOUGHTON MIFFLIN COMPANY
Evanston, Illinois   Boston   Dallas

ISBN-13: 978-0-618-13667-4   ISBN-10: 0-618-13667-3

14 15 16 - MDO - 12 11 10 09 08 07

Contents

Academic Vocabulary Lessons (continued)

Spelling Lessons

Vocabulary

Tools for Vocabulary Study

The *Vocabulary and Spelling Book* contains lessons designed to help you understand and remember important vocabulary skills and strategies. You will often need to use basic reference sources to master these new techniques and to complete the exercises within the book. Use the information below to help you in your work.

Using References

Dictionaries

A dictionary can tell you more than just what a word means. Look at the following dictionary entries to see some of the many details a dictionary can provide about a word.

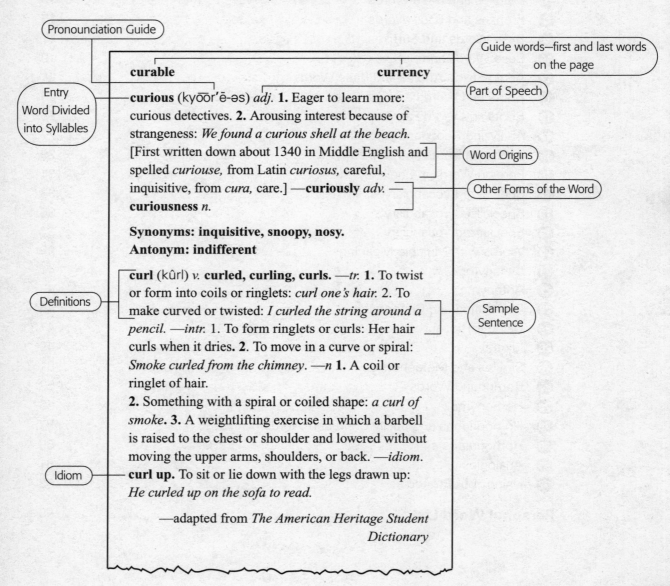

Pronounciation Guide

Entry
Word Divided
into Syllables

Guide words—first and last words
on the page

Part of Speech

Word Origins

Other Forms of the Word

Definitions

Sample
Sentence

Idiom

curable   **currency**

curious (kyŏŏr′ē-əs) *adj.* **1.** Eager to learn more: curious detectives. **2.** Arousing interest because of strangeness: *We found a curious shell at the beach.* [First written down about 1340 in Middle English and spelled *curiouse,* from Latin *curiosus,* careful, inquisitive, from *cura,* care.] —**curiously** *adv.* —**curiousness** *n.*

Synonyms: inquisitive, snoopy, nosy.
Antonym: indifferent

curl (kûrl) *v.* **curled, curling, curls.** —*tr.* **1.** To twist or form into coils or ringlets: *curl one's hair.* 2. To make curved or twisted: *I curled the string around a pencil.* —*intr.* 1. To form ringlets or curls: Her hair curls when it dries. **2.** To move in a curve or spiral: *Smoke curled from the chimney.* —*n* **1.** A coil or ringlet of hair.
2. Something with a spiral or coiled shape: *a curl of smoke.* **3.** A weightlifting exercise in which a barbell is raised to the chest or shoulder and lowered without moving the upper arms, shoulders, or back. —*idiom.*
curl up. To sit or lie down with the legs drawn up: *He curled up on the sofa to read.*

—adapted from *The American Heritage Student
Dictionary*

If a word has more than one meaning, how do you choose the right one?

Here's How

Choosing the Right Definition

1. **Rule out definitions that don't make sense,** given what you're reading about. If you're reading about a girl getting ready for a party, for instance, you could rule out the third definition of *curl.*

2. **Try adding words to the sentence** that go with each particular meaning of the word. In "Sasha has been doing curls at the gym," you could try "doing curls [in her hair]" and "doing curls [with weights]."

3. **Pick the definition that best fits the sentence.** In "Sasha wants to wear her hair in curls," the first definition for the noun form works best.

Thesauruses

A **thesaurus** is a dictionary of **synonyms.** Some thesauruses also include definitions, sample sentences, and **antonyms**—words that have opposite meanings to that of the entry word.

When you need to find a replacement for a word look up the word in the thesaurus. Entries are often listed in alphabetical order.

(Part of Speech)——**curl,** *verb*

(Definition) ⅃ **1.** To have or cause to have a curved, winding, or wavy form or surface. **syn:** *coil, corkscrew, snake,*——(Synonyms)
twist, weave, wind. **ant:** *straight, uncurl.*——(Antonyms)

(Synonyms)

Context Clues

Teaching

You often can figure out the meaning of an unfamiliar word from **context clues,** or information in the same or nearby sentences. In the following example, learning that the hikers found the waterfall by hearing, not sight, helps you understand the meaning of the word *invisible*—"unable to be seen."

> Deep in the forest, the waterfall was *invisible,* but the playful sound of rushing water led us to it.

A. Context Clues in Action

In the sentences below, use context clues to help figure out the meaning of the word printed in italics. Then write the meaning of the word on the line.

1. The squirrel hid in the tree and did not *emerge* until the people had left the park.

   meaning: _____

2. The second crash of thunder was much louder and closer than the *previous* one.

   meaning: _____

3. "That's *obvious*," he said angrily. "Anyone can see that it's raining."

   meaning: _____

4. Marta has excellent *posture;* she never slouches.

   meaning: _____

5. The sun and rain caused the dying plants to turn green and *flourish.*

   meaning: _____

6. The first time he skied down the hill without falling, José felt great *satisfaction*.

   meaning: _____

7. After the *truant* had missed six days of school, the principal called her parents.

   meaning: _____

8. The elevator stopped with a *jolt*, throwing everyone against the walls.

   meaning: _____

9. Learning the shape of the leaves is a good way to *identify* a tree.

   meaning: _____

10. When the four-year-old began composing music, people realized he was a *genius*.

    meaning: _____

Lesson 1 | # Context Clues

B. Vocabulary Words in Action

Review the meanings of the words in exercise A. Then read the following sentences. Write **T** if the sentence is true and **F** if it is false.

____ 1. The ending of an exciting mystery story is obvious.

____ 2. People usually feel satisfaction after finishing a hard job.

____ 3. A genius is less intelligent than other people.

____ 4. The previous page comes right after this one.`

____ 5. Graceful dancers always land with a jolt.

____ 6. It may be hard to identify a person wearing a mask.

____ 7. A living thing that does not flourish may die soon.

____ 8. When a rabbit emerges from its hole, it disappears below ground.

____ 9. A truant never misses a day of school.

____10. Standing up straight and tall leads to poor posture.

C. Vocabulary Challenge

Use context clues to figure out the meanings of the words in italics. Then circle the word from the three choices next to the sentence that has a similar meaning.

1. Marla was *absolutely* sure that she had been asleep, because the alarm woke her.   accidentally/completely/constantly

2. The doctor assured him that the results of the tests were completely *normal*.   confusing/unexpected/average

3. After reading the story, answer the questions on the *reverse* side.   opposite/front/related

4. "I won't accept that *feeble* excuse," her father said sternly.   believable/weak/funny

5. It's natural to *grieve* when someone you love dies.   eat sweets/sing softly/be sad

Restatement Context Clues   *Teaching*

Some context clues restate the meaning of a word in another way. **Restatements** are often introduced by commas or dashes and by words and phrases such as *or, that is,* or *in other words*. In the following sentence, the words between the dashes—*really, really angry*—restate the meaning of *indignant*.

   Anya was *indignant*—really, really angry—that the bus left without her.

A. Restatement Clues in Action

In each sentence below, use the restatement clue to help you discover the meaning of the italicized word. Underline the word or phrase that is a restatement clue. Then write the meaning of the italicized word on the line.

1. Martin knew he could *accomplish*, or do, whatever he set his mind to.

   meaning: _____

2. The field trip to the *poultry* farm—with its chickens, turkeys, and ducks—was fun.

   meaning: _____

3. The heavy *pulse*, or beat, of the rock music gave Sabine's mother a headache.

   meaning: _____

4. You have to be really *wealthy*—rolling in money—to have a private tennis court.

   meaning: _____

5. The decoration was so *elaborate*, that is, complicated and detailed, it made me dizzy.

   meaning: _____

6. Please *shred* the cabbage for the cole slaw by cutting it into long strips.

   meaning: _____

7. Thank you for doing such a *thorough*—really complete and careful—job.

   meaning: _____

8. Luis's father teaches *economics*, the science of money and what it buys.

   meaning: _____

9. It's easy to shop using a *catalog*, that is, a list of items for sale.

   meaning: _____

10. The race cars were so *rapid*—or fast—that they passed in a blur.

    meaning: _____

Lesson 2 Restatement Context Clues

| accomplish | pulse | elaborate | thorough | catalog |
| poultry | wealthy | shred | economics | rapid |

B. Vocabulary Words in Action

Review the meanings of the words in the list above. Then insert the correct word in each blank in the following paragraph.

Our trip to the _____ farm was a real treat. The owners gave

us a _____ explanation of how they feed and care for the

birds. I was surprised at how _____ the feeding process was.

The farmers _____ leftovers from their dinner and mix it with

corn and other seeds. Getting a chicken or duck to grow up healthy is not

easy to _____. It's a lot of hard work, and doesn't usually

make the farmer _____. Our host explained that the

_____ of his job is like being on a teeter totter. The

_____ _____ of changes in prices make life

really interesting, he said. Before we left, he gave each of us a

_____ listing all the products he offers for sale—from eggs to

baby chicks to Thanksgiving turkeys.

C. Vocabulary Challenge

The sentences below are missing restatement clues. For each item, choose the clue from the list that restates the word in italics and write it in the blank.

| twist and squeeze | soaked to the skin | dried grapes |
| strange and unusual | the teeth of a saw | |

1. My favorite cereal has lots of *raisins*, or _____, in it.

2. Beatrice had a dream that was as *weird*, as _____, as any science fiction story.

3. The *jagged* mountain peaks looked like _____.

4. The class was *drenched*—thoroughly _____—after the thunderstorm.

5. They actually had to *wring*, that is, _____, their clothes out.

Lesson 3

Contrast Context Clues

Teaching

Contrast clues are words or phrases that mean the opposite of an unfamiliar word. A contrast clue may be signaled by words and phrases such as *but, however, although,* and *on the other hand*. In the following sentence, the word *although* signals the contrast between the clue, a *small* scoop, and the meaning of *immense*—"huge."

> Benji helped himself to an *immense* portion of ice cream, although his mother had told him to take just a small scoop.

A. Contrast Clues in Action

In the sentences below, look for contrast clues that mean the opposite of the word printed in italics. For each item, underline the word or phrase that is an opposite of the word in italics. Then circle the best meaning of the word in italics from the three choices next to the sentence.

1. The *youngster* climbed under the fence, but her father had to use the gate.   gymnast   child   truant

2. Most people mow a lawn in straight lines; however, Carl made a *zigzag* pattern.   plaid   messy   back and forth in sharp turns

3. The *elder* sister wore a blue dress; on the other hand, the younger one wore red.   older   shorter   brighter color

4. You can *doze* in class again; however if you do, I'll pinch you and wake you up.   make a mistake   draw   fall asleep

5. The twins played a piano *duet*, but their brother did a trumpet solo.   piece for two players   melody   piece for one player

6. Although Sam's suit was *costly*, his shoes were cheap.   fashionable   expensive   valuable

7. "I don't have anything *decent* to wear. Everything's wrong."   dirty   interesting   proper

8. Cats are *beloved* animals to Dejan; however, his sister hates them.   tame   well-liked   friendly

9. Although the time in a dentist's chair is *brief*, it can feel like several hours.   short   painful   frightening

10. The *departure* of their flight was delayed for 20 minutes, but they still arrived on time.   destination   order   leaving

Contrast Context Clues

More Practice

| youngster | elder | duet | decent | brief |
| zigzag | doze | costly | beloved | departure |

B. Vocabulary Words in Action

Write the word from the list above that is most closely related to the italic words in each sentence.

1. Alicia wrote a special poem for her *favorite* aunt's birthday.   _____

2. The *price* of popcorn at the theater was *more than* admission to the movie.   _____

3. Emily avoided getting caught by running *back and forth across* the field.   _____

4. My parents put my sister in charge because she was *born two years before I was.*   _____

5. "It'll be *over before you know it*," the nurse said about the flu shot.   _____

6. After *napping*, Marge felt rested and ready to do her homework.   _____

7. "Thanks for inviting me to your party," Nora said as she was *leaving*.   _____

8. If we don't lock the cabinets, *my little brother* gets into everything.   _____

9. *Jane and Eric wrote a song and sang it* at the assembly.   _____

10. Sasha is always *polite and well-behaved*.   _____

C. Vocabulary Challenge

Read each sentence below, paying special attention to contrast clues. Then fill in the blank with the correct word from the list.

| deposit | backward | loosen |
| active | gorgeous | |

1. The male puppy slept a lot. The female, on the other hand, was very _____.

2. Jess thought the flowers were _____, but Amy said they were unattractive.

3. If you can't move forward, try going _____.

4. I wanted to _____ money in my account; however, I had to make a withdrawal.

5. Tightening the boot laces may not work. If not, _____ them a bit.

Lesson 4 · Definition Context Clues

Teaching

A common type of context clue actually defines a word that may be unfamiliar. A **definition clue** is similar to a restatement clue. Definition clues may be signaled by commas or dashes and words or phrases such as or, *that is*, and *in other words.* In the following sentence, the comma and the word *or* signal the definition of *props*.

> Everyone had a part in the play: some were actors, some did the lighting, and others were in charge of the *props*, or scenery and objects used on the stage.

A. Definition Clues in Action

In each sentences below, look for clues that define the word printed in italics. For each item, underline the word or phrase that is a definition clue.

1. The best team usually *prevails*—is the winner.

2. In this race, you have to *sprint*, that is, run as fast as you can.

3. Everyone experiences some *misfortune*, or bad luck, at one time or another.

4. Many states charge a *levy*—a tax—on items such as groceries and clothing.

5. Her mother's spaghetti is so good that Janine *devours* it, eats it all up, even if she isn't very hungry.

6. "Put away your books and get ready for a short *quiz*. Yes, that means a test."

7. Uncle Max *prefers* coffee to tea; that is, he likes coffee more.

8. All languages have *vowels*—open sounds—and consonants—sounds made by stopping the breath.

9. The *accordion*, a musical instrument with a keyboard attached to a squeeze box, has a lively sound.

10. To join our club, members must take an *oath*, or make a solemn statement, promising to keep our activities a secret.

11. Michael *anticipated*—expected—that he would receive a new CD for his birthday.

12. Angela thought the red and orange metallic wallpaper was *gaudy*, or showy in a tasteless way.

13. During their mountain hike, Zach and Hank came across a beautiful *cascade*, that is, a waterfall over steep rocks.

14. To enter school, students must first *register*, or officially sign up, in the Principal's Office.

15. Once part of an ancient sea, the Mojave Desert is known for its *arid*—really dry—climate.

Definition Context Clues

B. Vocabulary Words in Action

Circle the letter of the word that best completes each sentence below.

1. Sid feared he wouldn't pass the
   _____.
   a) levy   b) oath   c) quiz

2. Alice had trouble pronouncing her
   _____ when she got braces.
   a) accordion   b) vowels   c) cascade

3. Bob's father _____ to sleep
   late on Saturday.
   a) prefers   b) prevails   c) registers

4. Listening to the _____ can
   cheer people up.
   a) oath   b) misfortune   c) accordion

5. In a shouting match, the strongest voice
   _____.
   a) anticipates   b) devours   c) prevails

6. Most people would rather not pay a
   _____.
   a) misfortune   b) quiz   c) levy

7. _____ in that race was great
   exercise.
   a) Sprinting   b) Registering   c) Anticipating

8. When Jules broke his leg, people said they
   were sorry for his _____.
   a) misfortune   b) cascade   c) accordion

9. At the inauguration, the President takes the
   _____ of office.
   a) arid   b) vowels   c) oath

10. Lee is such a fast reader that he
    _____ a book a night.
    a) prevails   b) devours   c) prefers

C. Vocabulary Challenge

The italicized words and definition clues in the following sentences do not match
up. First, read all the sentences. Then circle the definition clues. Finally, match
each clue with the word it defines and rewrite the sentences on a separate sheet
of paper.

1. Pets are sometimes *abused*, or informed, by their owners.

2. The police should be *notified*—in the middle—when a car accident takes place.

3. The doctor prescribed an *oral* medication for my earache—in other words, one that is treated badly.

4. The orchestra concert was truly *wondrous*—given by mouth.

5. A *medium*, or amazing, size sweatshirt usually fits Evie best.

Comparison Context Clues

Comparison clues are words that mean the same as an unfamiliar word. These context clues may be signaled by words or phrases such as *like, as, similar to, also,* and *in the same way.* In the following sentence, the word *like* signals the phrase that means the same as *foliage*—leaves and flowers.

> The *foliage* in Jason's yard was like the leaves and flowers in a Japanese garden.

A. Comparison Clues in Action

In each sentence below, use the comparison clue to help you discover the meaning of the italicized word. Underline the word or phrase that is a comparison clue. Then write the meaning of the italicized word on the line.

1. Like foreign languages, *alien* foods, clothing, and customs take getting used to.

   meaning: _____

2. The weather *forecast* is an educated guess, in the same way that other predictions are.

   meaning: _____

3. Ancient *literature*, like later writing, deals with basic human activities and feelings.

   meaning: _____

4. Tanya's diet is so *strict* that she shows an athlete's discipline and control.

   meaning: _____

5. To *expand* your knowledge and broaden your understanding of the world, read as much as possible.

   meaning: _____

6. The darkness was so *intense* that the room resembled the inside of a cave.

   meaning: _____

7. The *gems* and other precious stones sparkled like a rainbow on fire.

   meaning: _____

8. If people didn't *differ* almost like snowflakes do, we'd all be very bored.

   meaning: _____

9. To make paste, *combine* flour and water the way you'd mix ingredients for cookies.

   meaning: _____

10. The *artificial* roses looked as fake as if they had been made by a child.

    meaning: _____

Name _____ Date _____

Lesson 5

Comparison Context Clues

More Practice

alien	literature	expand	gems	combine
forecast	strict	intense	differ	artificial

B. Vocabulary Words in Action

Review the meanings of the words in the list above. Then insert the correct word
in each blank in the following paragraph.

_____ can be absolutely fascinating. Their colors

_____ greatly—there's probably one for every shade of the rain-

bow. Even though some, like cultured pearls, are made by people, most of us

wouldn't call them _____. On the other hand, some stones are

so strange looking, you might think they came from an _____

planet. Jewelers cut precious stones so they give off _____ light

and sparkle brightly. There are no _____ rules in jewelry mak-

ing. A ring or necklace may _____ several colors and shapes. I

_____ that if you read the _____ about gems,

your appreciation for these beautiful creations of nature will

_____ greatly.

C. Vocabulary Challenge

For each item, choose the word from the list that best completes the sentence.
Use the comparison clues to help you. Then write the correct word in the blank.

author	former	hue	opposition	paradise

1. Oren's _____ house wasn't as large as the one he lives in now.

2. Lying on the sunny beach with nothing to do was like being in _____.

3. _____ to the mayor's plan was almost as strong as people's feelings against
   the new tax.

4. The _____ of the sunset reminded Amy of fresh, ripe peaches.

5. The best-selling _____ wrote tales similar to Aesop's fables.

10 VOCABULARY

Lesson 6

General Context Clues

Some context clues give more general information about a word. This information usually appears in the same paragraph as the word, but often not in the same sentence. In the following example, clues to the meaning of *systematically*—"in a careful, orderly way"—appear in the next sentence.

> Hoping to find his lost keys, Reynaldo searched his house *systematically*. He worked his way from the front to the back, looking in every room.

A. General Context Clues in Action

In each item below, look for clues to the meaning of the italicized word. Write the meaning of the word on the line provided.

1. When Jon was *ailing*, he had symptoms such as a fever, a stomachache, and chills.

   meaning: _____

2. Putting a grocery list in *alphabetical* order helps me remember it. So, for example, salt comes before walnuts but after celery.

   meaning: _____

3. You could hear Maurice's voice at the end of the hall. It was amazingly *powerful*.

   meaning: _____

4. I *wept* for days when my dog died. I missed him terribly and couldn't stop my tears.

   meaning: _____

5. I love the fresh smell of that new shampoo. It's wonderfully *fragrant*.

   meaning: _____

6. *Transparent* materials, such as glass, make a room seem larger because you can see right through them.

   meaning: _____

7. I can't believe how *stingy* you are. Can't I have more than one potato chip?

   meaning: _____

8. Joe kept his closet door shut. The *interior* was such a mess that he couldn't stand to look at it.

   meaning: _____

9. Helen's headaches are only *occasional*. She can go for months without having one.

   meaning: _____

10. "How much does it cost to mail a *parcel*?" "It depends if it's an envelope, a small box, or a large carton."

    meaning: _____

General Context Clues

| stingy | fragrant | alphabetical | transparent | ailing |
| wept | powerful | parcel | interior | occasional |

B. Vocabulary Words in Action

Write the word from the list above that is most nearly *opposite* to the phrase or words in italics.

1. Marla was interested only in how the *exterior* of her house looked. _____

2. The names were all *out of order* on the list, so no one could find her name. _____

3. The glass lid was *opaque,* which hid the contents of the box. _____

4. My brother has *never* missed a day of school because he was *ill.* _____

5. The team members *cheered* when they won the championship. _____

6. He gave me *papers* to be mailed. _____

7. Our gym teacher says we should get some exercise *every single day.* _____

8. My uncle bragged about his new aftershave, but I *couldn't smell it* at all. _____

9. Kayla's father is *generous* and gives her anything she wants. _____

10. The newborn puppy was so *weak* that it could barely stand up. _____

C. Vocabulary Challenge

Use example and other context clues to figure out the meaning of each word in italics. Then write a synonym for the word on the line provided. Use a dictionary if necessary.

1. When Marc stubbed his toe, there was a big *spurt* of blood. It looked like a miniature fountain.

   synonym: _____

2. He couldn't believe how *painful* the injury was. His whole leg throbbed.

   synonym: _____

3. He had to hobble around clumsily. He couldn't *flit* about like a butterfly any longer.

   synonym: _____

4. His whole foot would probably turn black and blue. It would be a *gigantic* bruise.

   synonym: _____

5. The experience put him in a *foul* mood. He snapped at people and was miserable.

   synonym: _____

Prefixes and Base Words

Teaching

Breaking a word into its parts can help you figure out its meaning. Two important word parts are **prefixes,** which are attached to the beginning of a word, and **base words,** words that can stand alone. The example below shows how a prefix can change the meaning of a word.

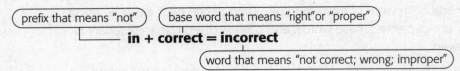

prefix that means "not"   base word that means "right" or "proper"

in + correct = incorrect

word that means "not correct; wrong; improper"

The chart below lists seven common prefixes that mean "not" or "wrong":

Prefix	Meaning	Example
dis-	not, lack of	disagree
il-	not	illegal
im-	not	imperfect
in-	not	incorrect
ir-	not	irregular
mis-	wrong, wrongly	misunderstand
un-	not, opposite	unsure

A. Identifying Prefixes and Base Words

For each word in Column A, draw a line between the prefix and the base word. Then match each example in Column A with its correct meaning in Column B. Write the letter of the correct meaning in the space provided. Use a dictionary if necessary.

> **EXAMPLE** mis|place   *k*

1. misguide _____
2. inactive _____
3. unfamiliar _____
4. illiterate _____
5. dishonest _____
6. impolite _____
7. mispronounce _____
8. irreplaceable _____
9. disinfect _____
10. unhappy _____

a. not truthful

b. having no substitute

c. to lead wrongly

d. unable to read or write

e. not cheerful

f. to destroy germs; to free from infection

g. not moving

h. to say incorrectly

i. not known

j. rude

k. to put in the wrong position; mislay

Lesson 7

Prefixes and Base Words

B. Prefixes and Base Words in Action

Prefixes: *dis-, il-, im-, in-, ir-, mis-,* and *un-*.

Underline ten examples in the passage that begin with the prefixes listed above.

Write the prefix and base word of each example. Then define each example using what you know about prefixes, base words, and context clues. Use a dictionary to check your answers.

Lenore was rarely irresponsible. However, one day she decided to explore the basement of her house. Her parents discouraged her from going down there because it was unsafe. The incomplete, unstable floor was home to many unwelcome pests. Lenore disliked the thought of running into spiders and snakes, but decided that being afraid was immature and illogical. She set out on her adventure. She made just one misstep, but that was enough. What do you think happened to her?

1. prefix: _____ base word: _____ meaning: _____

2. prefix: _____ base word: _____ meaning: _____

3. prefix: _____ base word: _____ meaning: _____

4. prefix: _____ base word: _____ meaning: _____

5. prefix: _____ base word: _____ meaning: _____

6. prefix: _____ base word: _____ meaning: _____

7. prefix: _____ base word: _____ meaning: _____

8. prefix: _____ base word: _____ meaning: _____

9. prefix: _____ base word: _____ meaning: _____

10. prefix: _____ base word: _____ meaning: _____

C. Vocabulary Challenge

For each prefix below, provide three different base words. Then write a sentence using one of the new words. Use a dictionary to check your answers.

EXAMPLE *im- possible, proper, patient*
Steve often becomes impatient in the checkout line.

1. *un-* _____, _____, _____

_____

2. *mis-* _____, _____, _____

_____

3. *dis-* _____, _____, _____

_____

Prefixes and Base Words

Teaching

Many words are made up of parts. Two important word parts are base words and prefixes. A **base word** is a word that can stand alone. A **prefix** is a word part that is attached to the beginning of a base word and adds to or changes its meaning.

(prefix that means "before") (base word that means "to see" or "to look at")

pre + view = preview

(word that means "to look at in advance")

The chart below lists seven common prefixes that express time, place, or direction.

Prefix	Meaning	Example
pre-	before	preheat
post-	after	postwar
mid-	middle	midsummer
re-	back, again	recall
sub-	under	submarine
super-	above, beyond	superhuman
trans-	across	transplant

A. Identifying Prefixes and Base Words

Add a prefix to each base word to create a word with the meaning shown. Then on a separate sheet of paper, write a sentence using each new word.

EXAMPLE *mid*term; an examination given halfway through a grading period
I had trouble with the midterm, but I did well on the final!

1. _____continental; across the continent

2. _____game; before the game

3. _____way; an underground method of travel

4. _____sonic; beyond the speed of sound

5. _____visit; to travel somewhere again

6. _____season; after the end of the regular sports season

7. _____washed; laundered beforehand

8. _____pack; to put in a suitcase or other container again

9. _____title; a secondary name or heading that appears below the main title

10. _____market; a store selling a wide variety of goods

11. _____term; a test in the middle of the year

Lesson 8

Prefixes and Base Words

More Practice

B. Prefixes and Base Words in Action

For each item, circle the word that makes sense in the story. Use the chart on the previous page and a dictionary to help you. Follow these steps to determine the meaning of each word:

• Divide the word between its prefix and its base word.

• Use your knowledge of prefixes and base words to predict the word's meaning.

• Use context clues to confirm your prediction.

I was so excited! It was my first (transatlantic, reissue) trip. I couldn't wait to fly across the ocean. I was going on my own, without (substandard, supervision). It was a (precook, predawn) flight, so I started getting ready at 2:00 A.M. I knew I wouldn't arrive until (return, midmorning), about 10:00 A.M. I brought some sugary, (presweetened, postdate) snacks in case I got hungry.

I had a real scare when I discovered a (transposition, transatlantic) of two of my passport numbers on my ticket. Instead of 6873, the ticket read 6837. I thought they would have to (supervision, reissue) the ticket, and I knew it would take time to write out another one. "Maybe they will (postdate, midmorning) it with the next day's date," I thought. Luckily, no one noticed the (predawn, substandard) way the ticket had been prepared. That was the beginning of my great adventure. What stories I'll have to share when I (return, transposition)!

C. Vocabulary Challenge

unite   star   register

Match each prefix with a base word from the list. Use each new word in a sentence. Use a dictionary if needed.

EXAMPLE super-*power*
Military and economic strength make the United States a superpower.

1. *pre-*_____

_____

2. *super-*_____

_____

3. *re-*_____

_____

Name _____   Date _____

Lesson 9

Base Words and Suffixes

Teaching

Some suffixes change the meaning of base words. Other suffixes add grammatical information such as the tense of a verb or the number of a noun. These suffixes are also called **inflected endings**. The spelling of a base word may change when you add an inflected ending. For example, you must drop the final *e* in *dive* before adding the suffix *-ing*.

(base word-verb that means "to fall headfirst")   (suffix that indicates ongoing action)

dive + -ing = diving

(word describing the action of a dive)

Study the common inflected endings listed in the chart below.

Suffix	Effect on Base Word	Examples
-s/-es	changes the number of a noun (from one to more than one)	ladder + *-s* = ladders, circus + *-es* = circuses
-d/-ed	changes verb tense (from present to past)	skate + *-d* = skated, walk + *-ed* = walked
-ing	changes verb tense (ongoing action)	sail + *-ing* = sailing, write + *-ing* = writing
-er	changes the degree of comparison in modifiers (more but not most)	sick + *-er* = sicker, easy + *-er* = easier
-est	changes the degree of comparison in modifiers (the most)	sick + *-est* = sickest, easy + *-est* = easiest

A. Identifying Base Words and Suffixes

For each example in Column A, draw a line between the base word and suffix. Then choose the correct definition of the word from the options given.

EXAMPLE saf/est   (a) the most safe   b) past tense of safe

1. geniuses   a) more than one genius   b) past tense of genius
2. escaping   a) in the process of an escape   b) more than one escape
3. called   a) past tense of call   b) in the process of a call
4. lighter   a) more light than something else   b) the most light
5. saddest   a) in the process of being sad   b) the most sad
6. answered   a) more than one answer   b) past tense of answer
7. washing   a) in the process of a wash   b) past tense of wash
8. clocks   a) past tense of clock   b) more than one clock
9. quicker   a) the most quick   b) more quick than something else
10. sunniest   a) past tense of sunny   b) the most sunny

VOCABULARY **17**

Name _____ **Date** _____

Lesson 9

Base Words and Suffixes

More Practice

B. Base Words and Suffixes in Action

For each item, underline the word that correctly completes the sentence.

1. I am not the (great, greatest) tennis player in the world.

2. English class is even (hardest, harder) than social studies.

3. (Swimming, Swim) is the sport I enjoy the most.

4. Dana (completes, completed) her science project last night.

5. Taking care of four (rabbit, rabbits) is a big responsibility.

6. What are you (thinks, thinking) about right now?

7. My room is (cleaner, cleaning) today than it was yesterday.

8. Ellie (practice, practiced) the violin for an hour yesterday.

9. Luke is the (taller, tallest) of all 15 boys in our class.

10. Two (students, student) were late to school this morning.

C. Vocabulary Challenge

Add two suffixes to each base word to create two new words. Use these suffixes:
-s/-es, -ed, -ing, -er, or *-est.* Then write a sentence using one of the new words.

> **EXAMPLE** base word *float*   new word *floated*   new word *floating*
>
> sentence: *Floating around in the neighborhood pool is my favorite activity.*

1. base word <u>join</u>   new word _____   new word _____

   sentence: _____

   _____

2. base word <u>light</u>   new word _____   new word _____

   sentence: _____

   _____

3. base word <u>rich</u>   new word _____   new word _____

   sentence: _____

   _____

Copyright © McDougal Littell Inc.

Lesson 10

Base Words and Suffixes

Teaching

A good way to approach unfamiliar words is to break them into their parts. Two important word parts are base words and suffixes. **Base words** are words that can stand alone. **Suffixes** are word parts that are added to the end of base words. Suffixes usually change the base word's part of speech.

(base word—a verb that means "to be angry") (suffix that means "full of")

resent + -ful= resentful

(adjective that means "full of anger")

Study the common suffixes listed in the chart below.

Suffix	Part of Speech	Meaning	Example
-ation/-ion	noun	state or quality of	imagination, reaction, competition
-er/-or	noun	one who	teacher, operator
-ness	noun	state or quality of	kindness, happiness
-ment	noun	state or quality of, action or process	amazement
-able	adjective	able to, wanting to, or being	acceptable
-ful	adjective	full of	restful, beautiful
-less	adjective	without	sleepless
-ly	adverb	resembling or in what manner	correctly, gently

A. Identifying Base Words and Suffixes

For each item, draw a line between the base word and the suffix. Then use the chart and your knowledge of word parts to predict each word's meaning. Check your predictions in a dictionary.

EXAMPLE   thank/ful (adjective) meaning: *full of appreciation*

1. joyful (adjective)   meaning: _____

2. leader (noun)   meaning: _____

3. strangely (adverb)   meaning: _____

4. agreeable (adjective) meaning: _____

5. temptation (noun)   meaning: _____

6. hairless (adjective)   meaning: _____

7. darkness (noun)   meaning: _____

8. hunter (noun)   meaning: _____

9. amusement (noun)   meaning: _____

10. subtraction (noun)   meaning: _____

Lesson 10

Base Words and Suffixes

More Practice

B. Base Words and Suffixes in Action

For each item, circle the suffix of the boldfaced word. Then use context clues and the chart on the previous page to predict the word's meaning. Use a dictionary to check your predictions.

1. My birthday was full of **excitement** and fun. meaning: _____

2. Brent wore sunglasses because of the **brightness** of the day. meaning: _____

3. Are those new shoes **comfortable,** or do they pinch? meaning: _____

4. Celia caught a cold that left her feeling tired and **powerless.** meaning: _____

5. It took three weeks, but I **finally** finished my science project. meaning: _____

6. My new camera develops pictures **instantly,** in the blink of an eye. meaning: _____

7. A local **banker** visited our class to talk about managing money. meaning: _____

8. "I'm **extremely** pleased with your behavior," said our smiling teacher. meaning: _____

9. Learning to skate can be **painful.** I fell at least 30 times! meaning: _____

10. I went in the wrong **direction**—east instead of west. meaning: _____

C. Vocabulary Challenge

Add two suffixes to each base word to create two new words. Then write a sentence using one of the new words. The spelling of some of the base words may change when adding a suffix. Use a dictionary to check your answers and spelling.

> **EXAMPLE** base word *color*   new word *colorful*   new word *colorless*
> sentence: *Terri made a colorful sketch using green, blue, and purple pencils.*

1. base word: move   new word: _____   new word: _____

   sentence: _____

2. base word: hope   new word: _____   new word: _____

   sentence: _____

3. base word: shy   new word: _____   new word: _____

   sentence: _____

Name _____ Date _____

Anglo-Saxon Affixes and Base Words

Teaching

Many common English words come from the language spoken by the **Anglo-Saxons,** people who lived in Britain about 1,600 years ago. Their language, Anglo-Saxon, or Old English, is the source of many modern English **base words**—words that can stand alone—and **affixes**—word parts added to the beginning (**prefix**) or end (**suffix**) of base words to form new words. Understanding these word parts can help you understand unfamiliar words and increase your vocabulary.

(base word from Old English *freond* that means "to love" or "to set free")

friend + -ship = friendship

(suffix from Old English *-scipe* that means "the state or condition of") (word that means "the state of being a loving person")

Study the common Anglo-Saxon affixes and their meanings in the chart below.

Affix	Type	Meaning	Example
fore -	prefix	before, earlier	foretell
mid-	prefix	middle, center	midnight
over-	prefix	above, superior	overpass
self-	prefix	oneself, automatic	self-control
under-	prefix	below, inferior	underground
-hood	suffix	state, quality, group	childhood
-ship	suffix	state, quality, group	hardship
-y	suffix	of, like, or tending toward	creamy, muddy

A. Identifying Anglo-Saxon Affixes and Base Words

Add a prefix or a suffix to each Anglo-Saxon base word to create a word with the meaning shown. Then on a separate sheet of paper, write a sentence using the new word.

1. _____-taught (having learned by oneself)

2. mother_____ (the state of being a mother)

3. _____sight (knowing events before they occur)

4. _____town (the center of a city)

5. _____pass (a passage beneath something)

6. _____less (unselfish)

7. owner_____ (the state of being in possession)

8. _____y (feeling drowsy)

9. _____fed (provide less food than needed)

10. neighbor_____ (a group of people living nearby)

Anglo-Saxon Affixes and Base Words   *More Practice*

B. Anglo-Saxon Affixes and Base Words in Action

foretell	*moldy*	*self-made*	*underscore*	*sugary*
midsummer	*overcome*	*understand*	*sisterhood*	*kinship*

Write the word from the list that best completes each sentence. Use context clues
and your knowledge of affixes and base words to help you.

1. Our family reunion is scheduled for June 21, or _____.

2. If you still don't _____ after reading the instructions, I'll explain the process again.

3. With so many obstacles to _____, it's amazing how well Darya has done.

4. Paul's dentist cautioned him about eating too many _____ snacks.

5. Someone who is totally _____ deserves all the credit for her accomplishments.

6. Yuri feels a real _____ with people who love music.

7. Sally's beach towel became _____ because she forgot to hang it out to dry.

8. One way to stress a word in your writing is to _____ it.

9. The girls in our class formed a _____ to discuss common ideas and problems.

10. Who can _____ what the future will bring?

C. Vocabulary Challenge

For each Anglo-Saxon base word, add an affix to form a new word. Then write a
sentence using the word.

1. bake _____

_____

2. word _____

_____

3. help _____

_____

4. partner _____

_____

5. child_____

Name _____ Date _____

Roots and Word Families

Teaching

Many English words are made up of word parts that come from other languages, especially Latin and Greek. These word parts are called **roots,** and their meaning is a clue to the meaning of the English word. Roots cannot stand alone, but must be combined with prefixes or suffixes. A group of words with a common root is a called a **word family.**

Latin root	Meaning	Word family
dic or *dict*	speak *or* tell	dictionary, dictate, prediction
form	form *or* shape	formation, transform, uniform
rupt	break	disrupted, interrupt, eruption
scrib or *script*	write	scribble, manuscript, scribe
trac or *tract*	pull *or* move	traction, tractor, distract
vid or *vis*	see	video, invisible, vision

The following tips can help you use roots to figure out the meaning of unfamiliar words such as *retraction*.

- Break the word into its parts: (prefix) re- + (root) *tract* + (suffix) -ion

- Think of other words you know that have the root *tract*, such as *attract* and *tractor*. Decide the meaning that they share—"pull."

- Think about the meaning of any prefixes or suffixes in the word: *re-* means "back" or "again," and *-ion* means "state or quality of."

- Put this information together to predict what *retraction* means: "something pulled back."

- Check the context and a dictionary or glossary to see if your guess is correct. In this case, you will learn that *retraction* means "something pulled back or in" or "the act of taking back a previously held statement or belief."

A. Identifying Roots and Word Families

Underline the root of each word in Column A. Then match each word with its correct meaning in Column B. Write the letter of the correct meaning in the space provided. Use the chart above to help you.

1. conform _____
2. visionary _____
3. subtraction _____
4. visit _____
5. disrupt _____
6. visual _____
7. reform _____
8. tractable _____
9. predicting _____
10. ruptures _____

a. saying beforehand, guessing
b. one who sees into the future
c. shape again
d. easy to move or control
e. the process of taking away from
f. breaks
g. to have the right shape
h. of or relating to sight; able to be seen
i. to break apart
j. to go to see someone

Roots and Word Families

More Practice

B. Roots and Word Families in Action

Predict the meaning of each underlined word following the steps listed on the previous page and using context clues given in the sentences.

1. The doctor wrote Raoul a <u>prescription</u> for pain medication. meaning: _____

2. Jan wrote a P.S., or <u>postscript</u>, at the end of her e-mail. meaning: _____

3. I love movies, so I want a career as a <u>scriptwriter</u> or a director. meaning: _____

4. Jeri's writing looks more like <u>scribbles</u> than recognizable letters. meaning: _____

5. My <u>prediction</u> that I would win turned out to be correct. meaning: _____

6. The <u>dictator</u> refused to let the people speak freely or vote. meaning: _____

7. My little sister has poor <u>diction</u>, so it's difficult to understand her. meaning: _____

8. The marching band was in precise <u>formation</u>—a perfect square. meaning: _____

9. My opinion is still <u>unformed</u>, but I will make up my mind soon. meaning: _____

10. The <u>formless</u> vase I made in art class won't win any prizes! meaning: _____

C. Vocabulary Challenge

For each item, write the root shared by the two bold-faced words. Then write the meaning of the root, using your knowledge of roots and context clues. Check your answers in a dictionary.

EXAMPLE   Sheila bought a **variety** of candy—every kind you can imagine.
The weather can **vary** in the mountains; first it's sunny, then it's rainy.

root: <u>*var*</u>   meaning: <u>*different*</u>

1. You can't control me—I want my **liberty!**

   The prisoners were **liberated** from jail and went home.

   root: _____ meaning: _____

2. Joe doesn't like to play football, but he enjoys being a **spectator** at our games.

   My mother **inspected** every inch of my room to see if it was clean.

   root: _____ meaning: _____

3. What an **incredible** storm—I couldn't believe how violent it was!

   Your stories don't have much **credibility** with me because you have lied to me in the past.

   root: _____ meaning: _____

Name _____ Date _____

Roots and Word Families

Teaching

A **word family** is a group of words that share the same **root**—the part of the word that gives its basic meaning. The meaning of the root, which often is Greek or Latin, can help you figure out the meaning of the English word. This chart shows some of the most common Greek roots, also called **combining forms**.

Greek Root/Combining Form	Meaning	Examples
auto	self, same	automatic, autograph
bio	life	biography, biohazard
cycl	ring, circle	unicycle, cyclone
graph	write, draw, record	photograph, graphic
log	word, study	psychology, logic
tele	far	television, telegraph

The following tips can help you use roots to figure out the meaning of unfamiliar words such as *biographer*.

• Break the word into its parts: (root) bio- + (root) *graph* + (suffix) -er

• Think of other words you know that have the root graph, such as *graph* and *autograph.* Decide the meaning that they share—"written."

• Think about the meaning of the rest of the word parts: *bio-,* "life" and *-er,* "one who is or does."

• Put this information together to predict what biographer means: "a person who writes about someone else's life."

• Check the context of the sentence or paragraph and a dictionary to see whether your prediction is correct.

A. Roots and Word Families in Action

Underline the root or combining form for each word. Then use the chart above and your knowledge of word roots to match each word in Column A with its correct meaning in Column B. You may also use a dictionary if needed.

1. automatic _____   a. the science applying engineering principles to living things

2. biochemical _____   b. an instrument for viewing distant objects

3. telepathy _____   c. able to govern itself

4. dialogue _____   d. circular

5. telescope _____   e. occurring by itself

6. bioengineering _____   f. of the processes taking place in living things

7 analogous _____   g. having the same properties as

8. cyclical _____   h. a machine that spins objects in a rapid, circular motion

9. autonomous _____   i. a conversation between two people

10. cyclotron _____   j. communication by extrasensory perception

Lesson 13

Roots and Word Families

More Practice

B. Roots and Word Families in Action

Predict the meaning of each underlined word following the steps on the previous page and using context clues given in the sentences. Use a dictionary to check your answers.

1. When I am a rock star, I will <u>autograph</u> albums for my fans. meaning: _____

2. Jenny's hands were covered in <u>graphite</u>. meaning: _____

3. A <u>seismograph</u> can record the strength of an earthquake. meaning: _____

4. The <u>graphologist</u> said that handwriting reveals personality. meaning: _____

5. Mara began writing her <u>autobiography</u> at seven. meaning: _____

6. I made a <u>graph</u> that shows the vote totals. meaning: _____

7. Once, the fastest way to send a message was by <u>telegraph</u>. meaning: _____

8. A <u>graphic designer</u> created the posters for the new play. meaning: _____

9. Have you ever listened to music on a <u>phonograph</u>? meaning: _____

10. I took eleven <u>photographs</u> with my new camera. meaning: _____

C. Vocabulary Challenge

For each item, write the Greek root shared by the two bold-faced words. Then write the definition of the root. Use a dictionary if necessary.

> **EXAMPLE**   The firefighter opened the **hydrant** to get to the water supply.
> Our town has a **hydroelectric** plant that uses a waterfall to make electricity.
>
> root: *hydr*   meaning: *water*

1. **Democracy** means government by the people.

   It's **undemocratic** to run the club without consulting the other people in it.

   root: _____   meaning: _____

2. **Phonics** is a way to teach reading that is based on the sounds of individual words.

   When Brad spoke into the **megaphone**, the whole crowd could hear him.

   root: _____   meaning: _____

3. Put an **asterisk**, a mark like this one *, by your first choice.

   An **astronomer** studies stars and planets.

   root: _____   meaning: _____

Analyzing Roots and Affixes   *Teaching*

Lesson 14

Base words are words that can stand alone. Other words are made up of base words or roots (word parts that cannot stand alone) and **affixes** (prefixes and suffixes). Breaking a difficult word into smaller parts can help you understand its meaning.

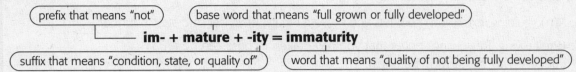

(prefix that means "not")   (base word that means "full grown or fully developed")

im- + mature + -ity = immaturity

(suffix that means "condition, state, or quality of")   (word that means "quality of not being fully developed")

As you can see from the example, base words sometimes change spelling when combined with other word parts. If you are unsure of the spelling of a word, check a dictionary.

Study the common base words, roots, and affixes in the chart below.

Prefix	Base/Root	Suffix
ex- (out *or* former)	guide	*-d, -ed* (changes a verb from present to past)
im-/in- (not *or* in)	mature	*-ation, -ion, -sion* (state or quality of)
mis- (bad *or* wrong)	pure	*-ing* (ongoing action)
pre- (before)	*plain, plan* (level *or* clear)	*-ity* (condition, state, or quality of)
re- (back *or* again)	*plaud-, plod-, plos-* (to clap)	*-ly* (resembling or in what manner)
	press	*-s* (makes a noun plural or a verb present tense)
	ten-, tend- (to stretch)	
	view	

A. Identifying Roots and Affixes

For each item, write the letter of the correct meaning in the blank. Use the chart above and your knowledge of word parts to help you. You may also use a dictionary if needed.

EXAMPLE reviews *d*

1. extends   _____   a. the state of being stretched out
2. plainly   _____   b. in a simple manner
3. maturing   _____   c. becoming fully developed
4. tension   _____   d. looks at again
5. premature   _____   e. steering or leading
6. guiding   _____   f. bursting violently outward
7 purely   _____   g. in a clean manner
8. repress   _____   h. stretches out; makes longer
9. impurity   _____   i. not yet developed
10. exploding   _____   j. push back
                                    k. the state of being unclean

Lesson
14

Analyzing Roots and Affixes

B. Roots and Affixes in Action

For each item, circle the word that fits the sentence. Use the chart on the previous page, context clues, and your knowledge of word parts to help you. You may also use a dictionary if needed.

1. A(n) (guiding, extension) cord lets you make a regular electrical cord stretch further.

2. (Previewing, Reviewing) notes that you have taken in class can be an effective way of studying for a test.

3. The (misguided, intending) ship sailed further and further off course.

4. The tractor was so heavy that its wheels made deep (plains, impressions), or dents, in the earth.

5. Is the water from the river clean enough to drink, or is it (reviewing, impure)?

6. I wish Roxane would act (maturely, expressly). Her childishness is so annoying!

7. (Plains, Pretends) are long, flat stretches of land.

8. It is important to let out, or (express, impress) your feelings, so that other people know if you are happy or sad.

9. Movie (extensions, previews) tell you about films that will be shown in a few weeks or months.

10. An (imploded, misplanned) star is one that has collapsed in on itself.

C. Vocabulary Challenge

For each item, add affixes to the root or base word to form two new words. Then write a sentence using one of the new words. Consult a dictionary to be sure that you are spelling and using the words correctly.

> **EXAMPLE** ambul (walk or go) _ambulance_ _preamble_
> _The ambulance sped through the city._

1. read _____ _____

_____

2. *strict* (to draw tight) _____ _____

_____

3. act _____ _____

_____

4. perfect _____ _____

_____

5. *serv* (serve) _____ _____

_____

Lesson 15

Analyzing Roots and Affixes

Teaching

Analyzing word parts is a good way to get an idea of a word's meaning. These word parts include **roots,** which are word parts that cannot stand alone; and **affixes,** which are word parts added to the beginning (prefix) or end (suffix) of base words and roots to form new words.

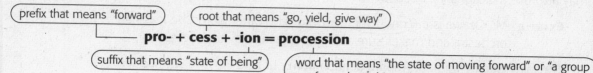

prefix that means "forward"   root that means "go, yield, give way"

pro- + cess + -ion = procession

suffix that means "state of being"   word that means "the state of moving forward" or "a group of people or things moving forward in an orderly way"

Study the common roots and affixes in the chart below.

Prefix	Meaning	Root	Meaning
re-	back *or* again	*cede/ceed/cess*	go, yield, give way
con-	with	*duct*	lead
de-	away, off, *or* down	*port*	carry
dis-	opposite	*tain*	hold
pro-	forward	*tract*	pull

Suffix	Meaning
-able/-ible	able to, wanting to, or being
-d/-ed	changes verb tense (from present to past)
-er/-or	something that *or* someone who
-ion	state or quality of
-ive	relating to, having to do with

A. Identifying Roots and Affixes

For each item, write the letter of the correct meaning in the blank. Use the chart above and your knowledge of word parts to help you. You may also use a dictionary if needed.

EXAMPLE detained _g_

1. distract _____
2. recede _____
3. tractable _____
4. proceed _____
5. deduct _____
6. production _____
7. deported _____
8. container _____
9. reduction _____
10. recessive _____

a. take away; subtract

b. to go forward

c. something in which material is held or carried

d. led away; forced to leave a country

e. to pull away from an original focus of attention

f. tending to go backward

g. held back; kept from leaving

h. the state or process of creating

i. the state or process of lessening or cutting back

j. to go back

k. able to be controlled

Lesson 15

Analyzing Roots and Affixes   *More Practice*

B. Roots and Affixes in Action

For each item, circle the word that fits the sentence. Use the chart on the previous page, context clues, and your knowledge of word parts to help you. You may also use a dictionary if needed.

EXAMPLE   Mr. Ozawa is a (conductor, deduction); in other words, he leads an orchestra and makes sure all the musicians play their parts well.

1. The rainy weather did not (report, detract) from our field trip—we still had fun.

2. I was (distracted, reduction) by the parade, so I did not notice you waving at me.

3. Megan's new CD player is (portable, proceeded), so she takes it everywhere.

4. The judge decided that the court should take a (conduct, recess), or break, for lunch.

5. A (porter, product) is someone who carries suitcases and other baggage.

6. A (concession, tractor) is used to pull farm machinery.

7. Your (conduct, portion), or behavior, has improved greatly this year.

8. When there is an economic (procession, recession), jobs become harder to find.

9. Steve has to wear a (retainer, traction), a device that keeps his teeth straight.

10. The student government meeting was extremely (detained, productive)—we discussed many problems and came up with plans to solve them.

C. Vocabulary Challenge

For each root, add an affix to form a word. Use the prefix and suffix charts on the previous page to help you. Then write a sentence using the word. Use a dictionary to check the spelling and meaning of the word you chose.

EXAMPLE   *mov* (move) <u>*remove*</u>
          It was hot outside, so I removed my jacket.

1. *flex* (bend) _____

_____

2. *pel* or *pul* (drive *or* push) _____

_____

3. *act* (do) _____

_____

4. *ject* (throw) _____

_____

5. *funct* (perform) _____

_____

Lesson 16

Foreign Words in English

Teaching

Many English words have been borrowed from other languages. These borrowed words often keep the pronunciation from their original languages, so it is often hard to predict how to pronounce such words. Context clues and a dictionary can help you learn their meanings and pronunciations.

> Pronunciation: -chet at the end of French words is pronounced /shā/

ricochet (rĭk′ə shā′) *intr. v.* **-cheted** (-shād′), **-cheting** (-shā′ĭng), **-chets** (-shāz′). To rebound at least once from a surface. **ricochet** *n.* The act of ricocheting. [French, from Old French, give-and-take.]

> Etymology (word origin): ricochet is a French word

Study the words in the chart below that have entered English from foreign languages. The words' pronunciations have been provided for you.

French	Spanish	Italian	Japanese	Dutch
boutique /boo-tēk′/	coyote /kī-ō′ tē/ or /kī′ ōt′/	confetti /kən-fĕt′ ē/	bonsai /bŏn′-sī′/ or /bŏn′-zī′/	coleslaw /kōl′ slô′/
bureau /byoor ō′/	patio /păt′ ē-ō′/	incognito /ĭn kŏg-nē′ tō/	hibachi /hĭ-bä′ chē/	sleigh /slā/
corsage /kôr-säzh′/	poncho /pŏn′ chō/	stucco /stŭk′ ō/	origami /ôr′ ĭ-gä′ mē/	sloop /sloop/
gourmet /goor-mā′/	tortilla /tôr-tē′ yə/	trio /trē′ ō/	sayonara /sī′ ə-när′ ə/	yacht /yät/

A. Identifying Foreign Words

Some textbooks and magazines use simplified respellings like the ones below. For each word below, circle the correct respelling. Use the charts on this page to help you.

Example trio a) TREE-oh b) tree-OH c) TRY-oh

1. boutique   a) BOO-teek   b) boo-TEEK   c) bow-TIE-cue
2. sleigh   a) slee   b) slay   c) SLEE-ig
3. hibachi   a) HIE-bah-chee   b) hib-BATCH-eye   c) hih-BAH-chee
4. incognito   a) in-cog-NEE-toe   b) in-COG-nih-toe   c) in-cog-NYE-too
5. poncho   a) PON-choh   b) pon-CHOH   c) PONK-oh
6. coyote   a) coy-OH-tay   b) coy-OH-tee   c) kie-OH-tee
7. origami   a) oh-RIG-a-mee   b) oh-ri-GAH-mee   c) oh-ridge-AH-mee
8. yacht   a) yagt   b) yassht   c) yaht
9. corsage   a) kawr-SAHZ   b) kawr-SAYGE   c) KOR-sahz
10. stucco   a) STOO-koe   b) STUCK-oh   c) stuck-KOE

Pronunciation Guide

ă p**a**t; oi b**oy**; ô p**aw**; th **th**in; ā p**ay**; ĭ p**i**t; ou **ou**t; th **th**is; är c**are**; ī p**ie**; ŏŏ t**oo**k; hw **wh**ich; ä f**a**ther; îr p**ier**; ōō b**oo**t; zh vi**si**on; ĕ p**e**t; ŏ p**o**t; ŭ c**u**t; ə **a**bout, it**e**m; ē b**e**; ō t**oe**; ûr **ur**ge; ♦ regionalism
Stress marks: ′ (primary); ′ (secondary), as in **dictionary** (dĭk′ shə-nĕr′ē)

Lesson 16 Foreign Words in English

More Practice

B. Foreign Words in Action

Underline the foreign word in each sentence. Use context clues to predict its meaning. Then check your definitions in a dictionary.

> **EXAMPLE** With his new glasses and beard, the spy was (incognito) even to his friends.
> prediction: *unknown* definition: *with one's identity disguised or concealed*

1. The new boutique carries the latest styles of clothes. prediction: _____

2. Our friends' yacht is like a floating hotel. prediction: _____

3. Let's grill chicken on the hibachi for supper. prediction: _____

4. I like the rough look of stucco on the walls. prediction: _____

5. The howl of the coyote echoed in the desert night. prediction: _____

6. Cole slaw is my favorite type of salad. prediction: _____

7. Yoichi waved and said, "Sayonara!" prediction: _____

8. Let's sit out on the patio and talk for a while. prediction: _____

9. Two horses pulled the sleigh through the snow. prediction: _____

10. The piano, violin, and clarinet trio played beautifully. prediction: _____

C. Vocabulary Challenge

For each item, circle the foreign word or phrase. Use context clues to determine which of the three definitions is correct, and circle the letter of the correct definition. Then look up the foreign word in the dictionary and learn its pronunciation.

> **EXAMPLE** My sister and her (fiancé) are getting married next fall.
>
> a) stranger (b) man who is engaged c) woman who is divorced

1. Samantha wants things to change, but I prefer the status quo.

   a) way things are now b) way things will be c) way things could be

2. Fred has such savoir faire; he always knows just what to do and say at a party.

   a) clumsiness b) ability to speak c) social know-how

3. I was persona non grata at the library after I made so much noise.

   a) an unwelcome person b) a friendly person c) a shy person

Specialized Vocabulary

Lesson 17

People who work in or study special areas of knowledge use a specific group of words, or **specialized vocabulary,** in talking about their subjects. For example, you might read the following sentences in an article about sailing or the ocean.

> The **lagoon**, or shallow pond, was as clear and smooth as a mirror.

> The circular formation of rocks surrounding the lagoon was a coral **reef.**

Since you don't hear or read specialized vocabulary as often as you do other words, look for context clues, such as definitions, restatements, or examples, to help you figure out their meaning.

- To figure out the meaning of *lagoon*, look for context clues in the sentence.

- Look for words such as *or*, *that is, in other words*, or *is/was,* that signal definition or restatement clues.

- Figure out that *lagoon* means "shallow pond."

A. Identifying Specialized Vocabulary

Circle the words or phrases that signal the definition or restatement in each sentence. Then underline the definition or restatement.

1. Face forward and stand on the **starboard,** or right-hand side, of the ship.

2. You'd be amazed at the variety of **aquatic** animals—that is, creatures that live in the water.

3. **Maritime** matters are ones that have to do with shipping or navigation.

4. We're sinking! **Jettison** everything, which means throw it overboard now!

5. A **submarine** is a ship that travels under water.

6. If you'll help lift, or **hoist,** the sails, we'll be on our way.

7. The **coastline** of Oregon, which is where the land meets the water, is spectacular.

8. The **lee** side of the ship is the side away from the wind.

9. Jeb has always wanted to be an **oceanographer**—in other words, a scientist who studies the oceans.

10. **Offshore** fishing, which is done far away from land, can be dangerous.

Specialized Vocabulary

More Practice

B. Specialized Vocabulary in Action

Read the paragraph. Then use the context clues to help you figure out the meaning of the bold-faced words. Write each word and its meaning on the appropriate line.

> Naomi has always been interested in **nautical** subjects such as ships and the ocean. Her grandfather was a sailor, or **mariner.** When she was young, he told her about his adventures as a **helmsman,** that is, the person steering a ship. He found his way through, or **navigated,** many bodies of water, from **shallow** to miles deep. He piloted everything **seaworthy** that would float, from flat-bottomed **barges** to pleasure **yachts.** He lived on the boats, cooking his meals in the **galley** and sleeping in a snug bed, or **berth.**

1. word: _____ meaning: _____

2. word: _____ meaning: _____

3. word: _____ meaning: _____

4. word: _____ meaning: _____

5. word: _____ meaning: _____

6. word: _____ meaning: _____

7. word: _____ meaning: _____

8. word: _____ meaning: _____

9. word: _____ meaning: _____

10. word: _____ meaning: _____

C. Vocabulary Challenge

Circle the specialized word in each sentence and underline the word or phrase that signals restatement or definition. Then write the meaning of the word, using the context clue as a guide. Check your answers in a dictionary.

1. For his project, Sam collected algae, which are simple plants found in water.

   word: _____ meaning: _____

2. To explore a beach safely, study the tides, or cycles of water levels.

   word: _____ meaning: _____

3. The water in a gulf is warm because it is partly enclosed by land.

   word: _____ meaning: _____

4. The keel of a boat is the part that runs along the bottom of the boat and keeps it from moving sideways.

   word: _____ meaning: _____

5. The mast, or tall pole that holds the sails of a ship, broke in half in the storm.

   word: _____ meaning: _____

Specialized Vocabulary

Teaching

The **specialized vocabulary,** or specific group of words, people use in talking about airplanes and flying may be unfamiliar. Sometimes comparison, contrast, and other clues in a sentence can help you understand such a word. In the following sentence, for example, look for a clue to the meaning of **altitude.**

> The **altitude** of a plane increases as it takes off, but it decreases when the plane lands.

- To figure out the meaning of *altitude*, look for words in the sentence that signal comparison, such as *like, as, also, in the same way*, or contrast, such as *unlike, on the other hand, but*, and *different*.

- Recall that a plane taking off gets farther away from the ground and one landing gets closer.

- Figure out that *altitude* must mean "height above the ground."

A. Identifying Specialized Vocabulary

Circle the words or phrases that signal comparison or contrast in each sentence. Then underline the comparison or contrast itself. Finally, write the meaning of the bold-faced word, using the context clue to help you.

1. The air was **turbulent** flying east, but very calm coming back west.

   meaning: _____

2. Like other people who drive vehicles, **pilots** must have good eyesight.

   meaning: _____

3. Airplanes are parked in **hangars,** just like cars are parked in garages.

   meaning: _____

4. To **taxi** down the runway, a plane moves much more slowly than it does once it's in the air.

   meaning: _____

5. Many people are as afraid when a plane **descends** as when it leaves the ground.

   meaning: _____

6. A **seaplane** is different from a regular plane because it can take off from and land on the water.

   meaning: _____

7. Unlike the **supersonic** SST, most passenger planes fly slower than the speed of sound.

   meaning: _____

8. Many early aircraft were **biplanes** similar to modern stunt planes with two wings.

   meaning: _____

9. The pilot sits in the **cockpit,** but the passengers ride in the body of the plane.

   meaning: _____

10. The **yoke** of an airplane is similar to the steering wheel of a car.

    meaning: _____

Lesson 18

Specialized Vocabulary   *More Practice*

B. Specialized Vocabulary in Action

Read the paragraph. Then use the context clues to help you determine the meaning of the bold-faced words. Write each word and its meaning on the appropriate line.

I think everyone would like to be able to fly. I actually did by riding in a **glider,** which is unlike planes that use **jet** engines or other motors for power. You just soar on the wind in an **aerial** ride different from any experience on the ground. The **take-off** is like riding a fast elevator. Unlike an airplane's liftoff, most gliders are **launched** by a plane that pulls them into the air. A glider has no **radar;** instead, your eyes are the only guidance system you have. Though you feel like a bird, you're really in an **aircraft.** The **airflow** around the wings is the same movement of wind as in a 747. The **touchdown** of a glider is also very similar to the landing of a 747. Controlling a glider makes you a real **aviator,** just like any other pilot.

1. word: _____ meaning: _____

2. word: _____ meaning: _____

3. word: _____ meaning: _____

4. word: _____ meaning: _____

5. word: _____ meaning: _____

6. word: _____ meaning: _____

7. word: _____ meaning: _____

8. word: _____ meaning: _____

9. word: _____ meaning: _____

10. word: _____ meaning: _____

C. Vocabulary Challenge

Circle the specialized word in each sentence and underline the comparison or contrast clue. Then write the meaning of the word, using the context clue as a guide. Check your answers in a dictionary.

1. Yukiko traveled only partway across the country, but her brother took a transcontinental flight.

   word: _____ meaning: _____

2. Like the speedometer of a car, the air-speed indicator of a glider measures how quickly a distance is traveled.

   word: _____ meaning: _____

3. Cargo travels in the same part of the plane as people, just under the floor.

   word: _____ meaning: _____

Name _____ Date _____

Specialized Vocabulary

The **specialized vocabulary,** or particular words, used in talking about measurement may be confusing. Use what you know about **context** (other information in the sentence) and word roots to help you figure out their meaning.

> Under a lens with high **magnification**, my eyelash looked like a redwood tree!

> Dolphins and bats use the echoes of sound waves to locate objects with **sonar.**

You can use the general context clues in these sentences to figure out the meaning of *magnification* and *sonar*, as shown below.

- The information that an eyelash looked like a tree means that it looked larger than it was. Therefore, *magnification* must mean "the process of making something look bigger." Knowing words with the same root, such as *magnify* and *magnifying glass*, can also help you determine the meaning of *magnification*.

- The information that sonar helps animals locate objects using echoes means that *sonar* is the location of objects by sound waves.

A. Identifying Specialized Vocabulary

Underline the information in each sentence that is a clue to the meaning of the bold-faced word. Think about whether you know any words with the same word root as the bold-faced word. Then write the definition of the word on the line. Check your definitions in a dictionary.

1. Alex used a **barometer** to measure the air pressure.

   meaning: _____

2. The **humidity** is so high that you can almost see the moisture in the air.

   meaning: _____

3. To find the **circumference** of a circle, measure the distance around it.

   meaning: _____

4. The instrument used to examine objects that are far away is a **telescope.**

   meaning: _____

5. A **microscope** magnifies very small objects so they are large enough to see.

   meaning: _____

6. Is the **volume** of that pitcher large enough to hold all this lemonade?

   meaning: _____

7. It's shorter to walk along the **diagonal** of a field than to go around two sides.

   meaning: _____

8. The light from a star 200 **light-years** away takes 200 years to reach the earth.

   meaning: _____

9. The very short waves of **ultraviolet** light are more harmful than visible light.

   meaning: _____

10. The **area** of a rectangle 4 feet by 2 feet is 8 square feet.

    meaning: _____

Specialized Vocabulary

More Practice

B. Specialized Vocabulary in Action

For each item, use context clues and your knowledge of word roots to help you choose the correct definition of the bold-faced word.

1. The car was traveling at a **velocity** of 35 miles an hour.

   a) speed   b) sound

2. Take a **linear** path home; I don't want to waste time traveling in circles.

   a) distant   b) straight

3. Don't just guess at the answer—take the time to **calculate** it.

   a) figure out   b) finish

4. Do you know how to **convert** inches into centimeters?

   a) answer   b) change

5. Light travels at the incredibly fast **rate** of 186,282 miles per second.

   a) brightness   b) speed

6. I ran three **kilometers** on Sunday.

   a) unit of weight   b) unit of distance

7. The **odometer** on my mother's car shows that it has been driven 98,000 miles.

   a) instrument that shows   b) instrument that shows time spent
      distance traveled

8. Tanya can **compute** complex math problems in her head.

   a) figure out mathematically b) memorize

9. Natalie used a ruler to **gauge** the amount of snow that fell this morning.

   a) move   b) measure

10. Scientists can only **estimate** the size of the universe.

    a) make a reasonable guess b) make a precise measurement

C. Vocabulary Challenge

For each item, figure out the meaning of the boldfaced word. Then on a separate sheet of paper write a paragraph of your own that uses all three words. Use context clues, your knowledge of word roots and prefixes, and a dictionary to help you.

1. It's important to take your measurements in a **logical** and reasonable way.

2. Your measurements are **inaccurate;** please do them again.

3. I **underestimated** how long my research would take, so I was at the library until late.

Words with Multiple Meanings

Teaching

Many English words have more than one meaning. Paying attention to context clues can help you figure out which meaning of the word applies in a particular sentence. The word *decree*, for example, has the following meanings: 1) an order that has the same force as a law, 2) the judgment of a court of law, 3) a ruling from a council in certain religious organizations, 4) to decide by decree, 5) to issue a decree. Notice how the word is used in the following sentences.

The court issued a **decree** regarding the election process. (Meaning 2)

Will the queen **decree** new taxes for her subjects? (Meaning 5)

A. Identifying Multiple Meanings

Read the multiple meanings of the two words given below. Then read each sentence and write the letter of the correct meaning of the italicized word in the blank.

land

a) the surface of the ground

b) to bring to earth

c) a country

d) to catch

e) a realm or area

fair

f) light colored

g) clear and sunny

h) just and equitable

i) lawful

j) promising or likely

____ 1. The baby's *fair* hair and dark eyes were a striking contrast.

____ 2. It's harder to *land* an airplane than to fly it.

____ 3. After a whole day on the boat, I didn't *land* a single fish.

____ 4. Deer are *fair* game in open hunting season.

____ 5. That's all for today from television *land*.

____ 6. Tomorrow's weather should be *fair* and warm.

____ 7. Alice didn't think that a 9:00 P.M. curfew was *fair*.

____ 8. Someday Dan would like to visit Italy, the *land* of his ancestors.

____ 9. The *land*, the sea, and the sky all seemed to blend together.

____10. Our team has a *fair* chance of winning the championship.

Lesson 20

Words with Multiple Meanings

More Practice

B. Multiple Meanings in Action

Complete each sentence with one of the two words given below. Then write the letter of the correct meaning of the word in the box.

express

a) to state in words

b) to show by gestures

c) to squeeze

d) direct and rapid

e) specific

nest

f) a bird shelter

g) to stack snugly

h) a comfortable home

i) a cluster of similar things

j) to settle into a safe place

1. "Did you have to _____ your anger by breaking a dish?" ☐

2. If you _____ the chairs, they will take up less space. ☐

3. Laura made her bedroom into a cozy _____. ☐

4. Please send the package by _____ mail, so I will get it tomorrow. ☐

5. The _____ purpose of Sara's exercise program was to tone her muscles. ☐

6. I'll just _____ here by the fire until the storm ends. ☐

7. For tomorrow, _____ your opinion of the short story in a three-paragraph essay. ☐

8. The first step in making lemonade is to _____ the juice from six lemons. ☐

9. The _____ of tables fits nicely into the corner of the den. ☐

10. The swallows built their _____ in our rain gutter. ☐

C. Vocabulary Challenge

Circle the word from the list that makes sense in both sentences. Use a dictionary if necessary.

1. light / mark / break / store

   Sometimes, all it takes is one lucky _____.

   _____ the candy into three pieces.

2. file / comb / burn / dress

   _____ your room to find the lost shoe.

   Fiona always carries a _____ in her purse.

3. swell / order / well / safe

   Your secret will be _____ with me.

   The burglar picked the lock on the _____.

4. turn / hit / hand / slip

   Please lend me a _____ with my homework.

   Let's give the actors a big _____.

5. mine / find / stuff / give

   This mattress has too much _____ in it.

   People will usually take all you can _____.

Synonyms

Words that are similar in meaning are called **synonyms.** These words have the same or almost the same dictionary definition, or **denotation.** However, they have different **connotations,** or ideas and feelings associated with them. Notice how the choice of synonyms makes the situation in the second sentence seem more serious than that in the first.

Marla and Marc got into a **dispute** over who should do the dishes.

Marla and Marc got into a **fight** over who should do the dishes.

Using a thesaurus (a reference book that lists synonyms) can help you choose the word that best expresses what you want to say.

A. Identifying Synonyms

Circle the synonym for each bold-faced word. Use a thesaurus if necessary.

1. This **parcel** is too heavy to go first class.

   postage/package/mail

2. Ellie's room is a **monstrous** mess.

   evil/abnormal/huge

3. Don't **brood** about your mistakes; just try to learn from them.

   worry/hatch/family

4. Karl felt great **anxiety** before his speech.

   care/eagerness/nervousness

5. The best **defense** is the truth.

   protection/guard/fortress

6. That old **vacant** lot is now a playground.

   blank/unpaved/empty

7. Vera did **thorough** research for her report.

   complete/thoughtful/absolute

8. Good doctors diagnose patients based on careful **observation.**

   celebrating/viewing/remarking

9. My mother spends her **leisure** time reading biographies.

   convenient/informal/free

10. I think the best **remedy** for a cold is sleep.

    cure/correction/revenge

Synonyms

More Practice

B. Synonyms in Action

sour—gloomy, angry, crabby, tart, wrong

decent—clothed, acceptable, agreeable, honest, so-so

Replace each use of **sour** and **decent** with the synonym that best fits the sentence. Use context clues to help you.

1. The flutist hit a **sour** note during his performance. _____

2. A **decent** person lives by the truth. _____

3. Did you just get out of the shower, or are you **decent** yet? _____

4. Megan was in a **sour** mood—she was full of sadness. _____

5. Evan loves **sour** fruit, especially lemons and limes. _____

6. The used-car dealer offered my mother a **decent** price for our old van. _____

7. Lisa was a really **decent** person, thoughtful and fun to be with. _____

8. Having a **sour** temper makes other people feel angry too. _____

9. You're so **sour** today that nothing will please you, will it? _____

10. Alan had a **decent** time at the party but would rather have stayed home. _____

C. Vocabulary Challenge

Circle the synonym that best completes each sentence.

1. Will you be (obtainable, available, qualified) to help with decorations for the dance?

2. You are wise to think of such a (cunning, evasive, false) plan.

3. I've told you (common, numerous, populous) times to stop doing that!

4. Please don't (mumble, chatter, lecture) to me about my faults; it hurts my feelings.

5. I think (old, senior, ancient) citizens have a lot of experience to share.

Antonyms

Lesson 22

Words that are opposite in meaning are called **antonyms.** Notice how the use of antonyms gives the two sentences opposite meanings.

    David **shunned** any outdoor activity.

    David **welcomed** any outdoor activity.

A thesaurus—a reference book that lists synonyms—often lists antonyms as well.

A. Identifying Antonyms

Using your knowledge of context clues, circle the antonym for each bold-faced word. You may also use a thesaurus if needed.

1. Rex is a **competent** skier, and he is getting even better.

    talented/competitive/unskilled

2. Anna treasured her **beloved** doll.

    despised/ragged/ugly

3. For your safety, please **heed** the warning signal.

    remember/ignore/repeat

4. My sore arm is sure to **impair** my performance at the swim meet.

    help/prevent/compete

5. Ida's coat is made of **genuine** leather—the real thing.

    handmade/expensive/fake

6. I'm **impressed** by your answer. Good job!

    disappointed/surprised/amused

7. The actor's new home was a **mansion;** it had 25 rooms.

    castle/condominium/shack

8. I performed better on the latest quiz than I had on **previous** ones.

    preceding/next/alternate

9. I have a **similar** idea, but it's not exactly the same.

    different/unknown/secret

10. The **timid** toddler stayed in his mother's arms.

    bold/quiet/frightened

Lesson 22

Antonyms

B. Antonyms in Action

For each item, choose the correct antonym for the bold-faced word. Use a thesaurus or a dictionary if needed.

sloppily	mature	primary	strict	neat
fresh	unfinished	rainy	destroy	despises

1. What you wear is a **secondary** matter; how you act is of _____ importance.

2. I **admire** Trey, but Allison _____ him.

3. The den is nice and _____ however, your bedroom is incredibly **messy**.

4. Sam's father is _____ but Sara's is very **lenient.**

5. This bread is **stale.** Where can I get some that is _____?

6. I **create** sand castles, but my little brother can only _____ them.

7. Is your homework **complete,** or is it still _____?

8. How **childish!** I wish he would be more _____.

9. Stella's work was done **neatly,** but mine was done _____.

10. Will the weather be **sunny** or _____ today?

C. Vocabulary Challenge

For each item, write at least two antonyms for the bold-faced word. Then use one of the antonyms in a sentence. You may use a dictionary or thesaurus if needed.

1. **tidy** antonyms: _____

   sentence: _____

2. **give** antonyms: _____

   sentence: _____

3. **warmth** antonyms: _____

   sentence: _____

4. **familiar** antonyms: _____

   sentence: _____

5. **clumsy** antonyms: _____

   sentence: _____

Denotation and Connotation

A word's **denotation** is its dictionary definition. A word can also make people feel or think a certain way. These feelings and ideas are the **connotations** of a word. Words with the same meaning can have different "shades of meaning"—that is, they can be understood differently.

> **Positive connotation:** Being on the track team has made Alan *slender* and *lean*. (attractively thin)
>
> **Neutral connotation:** Being on the track team has made Alan *thin*.
>
> **Negative connotation:** Being on the track team has made Alan *skinny* and *scrawny*. (unattractively thin)

Be sure that the words you use have the right connotation as well as the right denotation.

A. Identifying Positive and Negative Connotations

Each pair of phrases includes synonyms with different connotations. Put a **+** sign next to the one with a positive connotation and a **–** sign next to the one with a negative connotation. Use a dictionary or thesaurus if needed.

1. a powerful stink _____

   a powerful aroma _____

2. a dynamic leader _____

   a pushy leader _____

3. squandered his money _____

   spent his money _____

4. a reckless plan _____

   a daring plan _____

5. energetic children _____

   wild children _____

6. answered with arrogance _____

   answered with confidence _____

7. sloppy clothes _____

   casual clothes _____

8. an aggressive attitude _____

   a hostile attitude _____

9. an easygoing friend _____

   a lazy friend _____

10. a thoughtful response _____

    a calculated response _____

Denotation and Connotation

More Practice

B. Connotations in Action

In the first paragraph below, circle the words that have a positive connotation. In the second paragraph, circle the words that have a negative connotation. Use a dictionary or thesaurus if needed.

Positive connotation:

Ms. Baxter has been a(n) (valuable, costly) employee of this company for three years. In that time, she has expressed many (militant, strong) opinions. Her methods of solving problems are sometimes (unusual, bizarre). In short, she is a real (leader, show-off).

Negative connotation:

I was surprised to get a birthday gift from my Aunt Joanna. She is (an inquisitive person, a real snoop), so she had asked many of my relatives what I might like. I tore the (colorful, gaudy) paper off the package and found a shirt made of (flimsy, delicate) material. It was covered with (detailed, fussy) embroidery and (flashy, eye-catching) sequins. It certainly was a(n) (strange, exotic) present.

C. Vocabulary Challenge

Replace each word with a synonym that has positive connotations. Then write a sentence using the synonym correctly. Use a dictionary or thesaurus if needed.

1. nosy _____

_____

2. odd _____

_____

3. cheap _____

_____

4. overprotective _____

_____

5. glare _____

_____

Lesson 24 **Using a Thesaurus**

Teaching

Many English words are **synonyms,** or have similar meanings. To find the word that expresses exactly what you want to say, look in a **thesaurus,** or reference book of synonyms. A thesaurus entry will tell you the spelling, part of speech, and meaning of a word and its synonyms. To locate a word, look in the upper corners of the page for the **guide words**—or first and last words on the page. Words that come between those words in alphabetical order will be on that page.

conform ———— (Guide words—first and last words on the page) ———— **congratulate**

confusion, *n*. **Confusion, disorder, chaos, jumble** come into comparison when they mean a state in which things are not in their right places. **Confusion** suggests mixing of various sorts of things; **disorder** implies lack of arrangement; as in "His desk was in *confusion* (that is, with objects of all sorts mixed together), in *disorder* (that is, with objects out of place). **Chaos** suggests hopeless confusion. **Jumble** implies the mixing of incongruous things, as in "Their house was an architectural *jumble.*"

(Thesaurus entry for *confusion*)

(Part of speech—noun)

(Definitions that distinguish the synonyms, often with example sentences)

(Synonyms, may be presented in alphabetical order)

A. Understanding Thesaurus Entries

1. What are the guide words on this thesaurus page? _____

2. Would you expect to find the word *congratulate* on this page? _____

3. According to the entry, what part of speech is *confusion*? _____

4. According to the entry, what part of speech is *disorder*? _____

5. Which three synonyms of *confusion* suggest "objects out of place?" _____

6. Which word has the most general meaning: *disorder, chaos,* or *jumble*? _____

7. Which synonym of *confusion* fits best in this sentence? My desk is incomplete _____ I can't find anything.

8. Which definition do the three synonyms of *confusion* have in common—"lack of order" or "lack of distraction"? _____

9. Which synonym of *confusion* fits best in this sentence? That piece of art is a _____ of strange shapes.

10. Which synonyms of *confusion* is closest in meaning to *hysteria*? _____

Lesson 24

Using a Thesaurus

More Practice

B. Thesaurus Entries in Action

Read the following entries from the page of a thesaurus. Then choose a more exact synonym to replace the underlined word in each sentence. Write the word in the blank.

question, *v.* **Question, ask, interrogate, examine, query, inquire, quiz** come into comparison when they mean the act of seeking information. **Question, ask, query,** and **inquire** are broad, general terms. **Quiz** implies authority or threat; **interrogate** implies extreme threat or assumption of guilt. **Examine** implies a critical look.

neglect, *v.* **Neglect, omit, ignore, forget** come into comparison when they mean to pass over without proper attention. **Neglect** implies intentional or unintentional failure to pay attention, as in, "Don't *neglect* to pay

your rent." **Ignore** implies intentional disregard. **Omit** implies leaving out part of a whole, as in, "*Omit* the last chapter and concentrate on the first three." **Forget** stresses loss of memory.

common, *adj.* **Common, ordinary, popular, familiar** come into comparison when they mean being of a generally known character. **Common** implies the lack of distinguishing qualities, as in, "That's a very *common error.*" **Ordinary** implies being in the regular order of things. **Familiar** stresses being generally known or easily recognized; **popular** expresses widespread favor.

_____ 1. At our next meeting, we will <u>question</u> our club rules.

_____ 2. It may rain, so don't <u>neglect</u> to bring your raincoat.

_____ 3. His face is so <u>common</u> that I know I've seen him before.

_____ 4. If you <u>neglect</u> your last name on your paper, your test will be discarded.

_____ 5. My mother is sure to <u>question</u> me for hours about the broken vase.

_____ 6. That <u>common</u> song is on every radio station this month.

_____ 7. To <u>neglect</u> traffic signals is to ask for trouble.

_____ 8. How could you <u>neglect</u> that our report is due today?

_____ 9. It was just a <u>common</u> day, with nothing unusual happening.

_____ 10. Where may I <u>question</u> about a lost umbrella?

C. Vocabulary Challenge

Read the passage and substitute a synonym for each underlined word. Use a thesaurus if needed.

Ana decided to <u>receive</u> the offer of a scholarship to summer music camp. The camp director came to <u>receive</u> Ana when she arrived. The director showed Ana to her cabin and told her to <u>place</u> her violin on her bunk. Ana hoped that music camp would be the <u>place</u> to improve her skills as a violinist.

1. receive—synonym _____   3. place—synonym _____

2. receive—synonym _____   4. place—synonym _____

Idioms

Teaching

An **idiom** is a phrase that has a special meaning different from the meanings of the individual words. Notice how the idiom *ran out of gas* efficiently conveys the idea of being very tired.

> After working for three hours, I just **ran out of gas.**

> After working for three hours, I just **got so tired that I couldn't go on.**

The chart below lists some common idioms and their meanings.

Idiom	Meaning
A. all thumbs	very clumsy
B. as light as a feather	almost weightless
C. bark up the wrong tree	be mistaken
D. drop the ball	fail to follow through
E. fly off the handle	lose control
F. get cold feet	be afraid to do something
G. green with envy	extremely jealous
H. hit the nail on the head	be exactly right
I. open up a can of worms	begin something that should be left alone
J. put on one's thinking cap	think seriously

A. Identifying Idioms

Complete each sentence using an idiom from the chart. Each idiom is used only once. Write the letter of the correct idiom in the space provided. You may need to mentally adjust verb tenses or make other grammatical changes so that the idiom fits the sentence.

1. I am disappointed in Sheila. She really _____ when she didn't finish the project.

2. Jerry stood at the end of the diving board, but _____ at the last minute.

3. Stan is so strong that he thinks the 50-pound weights are _____.

4. I'm sure you can figure out the answer if you just _____.

5. If you think Mom will let you go mountain climbing without adult supervision, you are _____.

6. When Emma tried to thread a needle, she proved she was _____.

7. If you even mention that subject, you will _____ that nobody wants to deal with.

8. I know you're angry at me, but you don't have to _____.

9. Owen's new bicycle made his sister _____. She wishes she had one!

10. That answer really _____; I couldn't agree more.

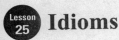

Idioms

B. Idioms in Action

Find ten idioms in the following paragraph. Write each and then define it. Use a dictionary if needed.

> Okay, let's stop beating around the bush. I know you don't like to get your hands dirty, but we all have to put our noses to the grindstone if the job's going to get done. Why is it so hard for you to just bite the bullet and get down to business? You seem to have a chip on your shoulder and be out to lunch most of the time. It's like pulling teeth to even get you to give me the time of day. Just climb on the bandwagon, will you?

1. idiom: _____ meaning: _____

2. idiom: _____ meaning: _____

3. idiom: _____ meaning: _____

4. idiom: _____ meaning: _____

5. idiom: _____ meaning: _____

6. idiom: _____ meaning: _____

7. idiom: _____ meaning: _____

8. idiom: _____ meaning: _____

9. idiom: _____ meaning: _____

10. idiom: _____ meaning: _____

C. Vocabulary Challenge

Replace each incorrect idiom with a correct one. Then define the correct idiom. Use a dictionary if needed.

1. Martin had the answer on the tip of his nostril, but Lucy said it first.

   idiom and definition: _____

   _____

2. Ethelyn was as busy as a buffalo preparing for the holidays.

   idiom and definition: _____

   _____

3. Although Bob acted as cool as a watermelon, he was actually nervous.

   idiom and definition: _____

   _____

4. Pam has two left elbows when it comes to dancing.

   idiom and definition: _____

   _____

5. They expect me to pull a rabbit out of my sleeve at a moment's notice.

   idiom and definition: _____

   _____

50 VOCABULARY

Lesson 26 Similes and Metaphors

Teaching

You can paint strong word pictures by comparing two things that share some qualities. A **simile** is a comparison of two things that have some quality in common. A simile contains a word such as *like, as, resembles,* or *than.* A **metaphor** is a comparison of two things that does not use *like, as, resembles,* or *than.* Instead, it states that one thing actually is something else.

I stared at the jacket **as** if it were an enemy.	*Simile*
The jacket was **like** a bad dream that never left me.	*Simile*
That jacket had become the annoying brother who tagged along wherever I went.	*Metaphor*

Comparison	Characteristics	Things Compared
Simile	With *like* or as	jacket / enemy or bad dream
Metaphor	Without *like* or as	jacket / annoying, tag-along brother

A. Identifying Similes and Metaphors

Underline the two items being compared in each sentence. Then write **S** if the comparison is a simile and **M** if it is a metaphor.

_____ 1. The library is as quiet as the bottom of the ocean.

_____ 2. Max's dog looked like a pile of mashed potatoes curled up on the rug.

_____ 3. When his headache began, Sam was a nail being pounded with a hammer.

_____ 4. Mila's polished nails look like frozen blobs of ketchup on her fingers.

_____ 5. When he gets angry, my grandfather is a fire-breathing dragon.

_____ 6. The snowfall was a shower of fluffy confetti.

_____ 7. Vince's feet resemble bumper cars.

_____ 8. The grass is a carpet of green velvet.

_____ 9. Ted's room is messier than a junkyard.

_____ 10. It was so cold that her teeth clattered like fingers on a keyboard.

Similes and Metaphors

More Practice

B. Similes and Metaphors in Action

Identify each sentence as a simile or a metaphor. Then explain the meaning of the comparison.

1. My mother swooped down on my misbehaving brother like a fighter pilot.
(simile / metaphor)

    meaning: _____

2. When I'm afraid, my heart sounds like a pair of sneakers in a clothes dryer.
(simile / metaphor)

    meaning: _____

3. Her eyes were lovely blue lakes.
(simile / metaphor)

    meaning: _____

4. Marianne is a library of sports facts and figures. (simile / metaphor)

    meaning: _____

5. His socks smelled like moldy cheese.
(simile / metaphor)

    meaning: _____

6. The storm was a black curtain.
(simile / metaphor)

    meaning: _____

7. She was angrier than a nest full of hornets.
(simile / metaphor)

    meaning: _____

8. Evan's bed was an island of peace in a stormy sea. (simile / metaphor)

    meaning: _____

9. That excuse is as flimsy as gauze.
(simile / metaphor)

    meaning: _____

10. The dancer moved around the stage like a marionette attached to strings.
(simile / metaphor)

    meaning: _____

C. Vocabulary Challenge

Complete each sentence by writing a simile or metaphor as indicated. Then write the meaning of your comparison.

1. Metaphor: Old chewing gum is _____

    meaning: _____

2. Metaphor: Sheila, the prettiest girl in the class, was _____

    meaning: _____

3. Simile: Brussels sprouts taste _____

    meaning: _____

4. Simile: Losing the championship game hurt _____

    meaning: _____

5. Metaphor: Love is _____

    meaning: _____

Compound Words

Lesson 27

Teaching

A **compound word** is two or more words joined to name a single object, idea, action, or quality.

> **sleepwalk** (verb) to move about or perform tasks while asleep or in a sleeplike state

Breaking a compound word into its base words can help you figure out its meaning. Compound words can be written as a single word, as a hyphenated word, or as two separate words.

> vineyard = vine + yard
>
> mother-in-law = mother + in + law
>
> sleeping bag = sleeping + bag

A. Identifying Compound Words

Complete the chart below by breaking each compound word into its base words. Then write the meaning of the compound word, using a dictionary if needed. Finally, complete the sentences using the correct word from the chart.

Compound word	Base words	Meaning
baseball		
teenage		
sunbathe		
self-conscious		
roller skate		

1. Standing in front of the class to give my report made me feel very _____ _____

2. A _____ _____ girl or boy should be allowed more freedom than a young child.

3. I decided not to _____ _____ anymore after I got a painful burn.

4. Andrew plays football in the fall and _____ _____ in the spring.

5. Be sure to wear a helmet, elbow pads, and knee pads when you _____ _____ .

Lesson 27

Compound Words

More Practice

B. Compound Words in Action

For each word below, add one or more words to form a compound word. Then write a sentence using each compound word correctly. Use a dictionary if you need to check whether the compound word you use is spelled as one word, as more than one word, or with a hyphen.

1. ice_____ _____

2. _____room _____

3. paper_____ _____

4. brother_____ _____

5. self_____ _____

6. _____way _____

7. _____friend _____

8. lightning_____ _____

9. news_____ _____

10. _____boat _____

C. Vocabulary Challenge

Circle the ten compound words in the following paragraph. Then write their meanings on the lines.

What an exciting time we had at the seashore on my birthday. We water-skied in the afternoon and then climbed the lighthouse to watch the sunset. It was a many-sided experience that Dad captured for our photo album. I hope to share the pictures with my great-grandchildren someday.

_____   _____

_____   _____

_____   _____

_____   _____

_____   _____

_____   _____

Lesson 28

Homonyms

Teaching

Words that are spelled and pronounced the same but have different meanings are called **homonyms**. Homonyms are listed in the dictionary in separate numbered entries. Each entry may have multiple meanings. The dictionary entry for two homonyms of *stoop*, for example, is shown below:

stoop[1] **1.** to bend forward from the waist, **2.** to sag, **3.** a forward bending of a person's head and back

stoop[2] a small porch or staircase that leads to the entrance of a house

Marla's grandfather walked with a **stoop.**

He liked to sit on the **stoop** and watch the sun set.

A. Identifying Homonyms

Circle the homonyms in each pair of sentences. Then write a brief definition of each word. Use a dictionary if needed.

1. Mara played third base on the team.

_____

   He was a nasty, base person.

_____

2. I never knew anyone so mean.

_____

   Do you know what I mean?

_____

3. He spoke in the imperative mood.

_____

   That put me in a bad mood.

_____

4. He would tell a huge lie.

_____

   Then he'd lie there and smile.

_____

5. She would pat you on the back.

_____

   She thought he had it all down pat.

_____

6. He'd like to keep people in a box.

_____

   He'd box with you if you disagreed.

_____

7. His cat would lap its milk.

_____

   But it wouldn't sit in his lap.

_____

8. Ann's dog was afraid to bark.

_____

   It just chewed on tree bark.

_____

9. I wouldn't pick him as a friend.

_____

   I'd rather dig a hole with a pick.

_____

10. I will try to forget him.

_____

   She left a last will and testament.

_____

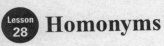

Homonyms

B. Homonyms in Action

For each item, choose the homonym from the list that makes sense in both sentences and write it in the blanks. Use a dictionary if needed.

1. bank / drove / port / bluff

   It's dangerous to play along the river _____.

   Put your money in the _____ first.

2. knot / pore / stand / order

   Lea had to _____ over the application.

   The effort clogged a(n) _____ on her chin.

3. polish / slap / smash / pitch

   Wind up before you _____ the ball.

   _____ is often used to waterproof roofs.

4. stem / skin / pit / dump

   Don't throw the cherry _____ on the floor.

   Please put it in the garbage _____.

5. story / novel / educational / odd

   Here's a(n) _____ idea for you.

   Why not read a(n) _____ just for fun?

6. hand / deck / spade / suit

   In many card games the last step is to lay down your _____.

   Hold your _____ up or I'll be able to see your cards.

7. heel / pile / loaf / slice

   All I've done is _____ around all day.

   I'm hungry enough to eat a _____ of bread.

8. sink / story / turn / list

   The ship began to _____ to one side.

   The captain made a _____ of all the damage.

9. boat / net / game / hold

   We had caught six fish in our _____ by 9:00 A.M.

   Our _____ catch for the day was 11 tuna.

10. jam / bread / slip / roll

    Tim had to _____ on the brakes to avoid an accident.

    The peanut butter and _____ ended up on the floor of the car.

C. Vocabulary Challenge

Read the definitions given and identify the homonym. Then use each in one sentence. Use a dictionary if needed.

EXAMPLE   to hit something lightly / a faucet   homonyms: *tap*
Tap on the wall when you see the water come out the tap.

1. the day, month, and year / a sweet fruit with a hard seed   homonym: _____

   sentence: _____

2. student / part of the eye   homonym: _____

   sentence: _____

3. an identifying label / a child's running game   homonym: _____

   sentence: _____

Name _____   Date _____

Lesson 29

Homophones and Easily Confused Words

Teaching

Many sets of English words sound the same but have different spellings and meanings. These sets of words are called homophones, from the Greek words *homos*, meaning "same," and *phonos*, meaning "sound."

Word	Pronunciation	Meaning
heard	hurd	(past tense verb) received a sound through the ears
herd	hurd	(noun) a group of animals that stay together, such as elephants

Homophones can lead to spelling mistakes. You may mean, "I heard the new song," but if you write "I herd the new song," you have made a spelling error. Here are other examples of homophones.

be (to exist), bee (an insect that makes honey)

flour (an ingredient in bread), flower (blossom)

here (in this place), hear (to detect a sound)

one (1), won (was victorious)

our (belonging to us), hour (60 minutes)

passed (went by), past (previous times)

by (next to), buy (purchase), bye (short form of *goodbye*)

there (in that place), they're (they are), their (belonging to them)

A. Identifying Homophones

Circle the homophones in each sentence. Then write a brief definition of each word. Use a dictionary if needed.

1. Do you know why there is no sunshine?

   _____

2. Oh, no—I must pay you the money I owe!

   _____

3. Adam sent his mother flowers that had a strong scent.

   _____

4. Would you like to eat just one pear, or would you prefer a pair of them?

   _____

5. Whether you print or write a word, always make sure the spelling is right.

   _____

6. I have felt tired and weak all week long.

   _____

7. Ted offered Barbara some peaches, and she ate eight of them.

   _____

8. If you will wait just a moment, you can get on the scale and find out your weight.

   _____

9. Shane made a jump of six feet and was awarded a medal for his amazing feat.

   _____

10. If you're not careful, you will hurt your leg.

   _____

VOCABULARY **57**

Lesson 29

Homophones and Easily Confused Words

More Practice

B. Homophones in Action

steal / steel   plane / plain   gnu / new   nose / knows   reel / real

rows / rose   tail / tale   shoo / shoe   stair / stare   there / they're

Answer each riddle using a pair of homophones from the list above. You may have to switch the order of the words. Use a dictionary if needed.

1. How do you get rid of footwear? _____ _____

2. What do you say when those people get where they're going? _____ _____

3. What do you call a story about the part of a dog that wags? _____ _____

4. What is a name for genuine fishing equipment? _____ _____

5. What are columns of red flowers? _____ _____

6. How do you rob someone's strong metal? _____ _____

7. What do you call an aircraft that has no decoration? _____ _____

8. What do you say when you recognize a smell? _____ _____

9. How do you describe a long look at a series of steps? _____ _____

10. What do you call a baby antelope? _____ _____

C. Vocabulary Challenge

The following paragraph includes five misspelled homophones. Read the passage and circle the incorrect words. Then write the correct words on the lines. Use a dictionary if needed.

It was my birthday, and I was expecting a lot of presence. Several of my friends past by my house, but no one came in. "There not mad at me, are they?" I wondered. "I'm already for a big party, and no one wants to come. Treating me like this shouldn't be aloud!"

_____ _____ _____

_____ _____

Name _____ Date _____

Homographs

Teaching

Many sets of English words are spelled the same but have different pronunciations and meanings. These sets of words are called **homographs**, from the Greek words *homos*, meaning "same," and *graphos*, meaning "written." They are often listed in separate numbered entries in the dictionary.

Homograph	Pronunciation	Part of Speech	Meaning
content[1]	kŏn′ tĕnt	noun	what is contained in something
content[2]	kən-tĕnt′	adjective	satisfied

The **content** of the package was a surprise to everyone.
Max was very **content** with the gift it held.

A. Identifying Homographs

Read each pair of sentences aloud. Then circle the correct pronunciation of each bold-faced homograph. You can also use a dictionary if needed.

EXAMPLE (târ, ⓣîr, tīr) Alex was not crying yet, but I saw a **tear** in his eye.
(ⓣâr, tîr, tīr) This shirt is ruined—there is a huge **tear** in the sleeve!

1. (băs, bās, bäs) Leo enjoys fishing for **bass** and trout.
   (băs, bās, bäs) Leo's brother plays the **bass** in the orchestra.

2. (clŏs, clōs, clōz) Please **close** the door so the dog doesn't get out.
   (clŏs, clōs, clōz) You're too **close** to the edge of the cliff!

3. (dŭz, dōz, dôz) Whatever he **does,** we wish him luck.
   (dŭz, dōz, dôz) Two **does** and their fawns just crossed the road.

4. (rĭ-kôrd′, rĕk′ ərd, rĭ-kûrd′) I want to **record** the interview so I'll know exactly what we said.
   (rĭ-kôrd′, rĕk′ uhrd, rĭ-kûrd′) I'll also take notes so we'll have a written **record** of the conversation.

5. (sōō′ ər, sō′ ər, sô′ ər) If I were a better **sewer**, I would make my own clothes.
   (sōō′ ər, sō′ ər, sô′ ər) Our **sewer** overflowed during the heavy rain last week.

6. (prĕz′ ənt, prĭ-zĕnt′, prĭ′-zĕnt) I have to **present** my report in science class tomorrow.
   (prĕz′ ənt, prĭ-zĕnt′, prĭ′-zĕnt) My favorite birthday **present** was a skateboard.

7. (lēd, lĕd, līd) The drum major had to **lead** the band when the conductor was ill.
   (lēd, lĕd, līd) I was so tired that my legs felt like they were made of **lead.**

8. (bō, bōu, bö) Be sure to **bow** to the audience after singing your song.
   (bō, bōu, bö) If you tie your shoelaces in a double **bow,** they won't come loose.

9. (dŭv, dōv, dôv) Hillary **dove** right into the cold water.
   (dŭv, dōv, dôv) The **dove** is a close relation to the pigeon.

10. (mĭn′ ĭt, mī-nōōt′, mī′-nōōt) Hold your horses; I'll be there in a **minute.**
    (mĭn′ ĭt, mī-nōōt′, mī′-nōōt) The crack in the glass was so **minute** that I could hardly see it.

Pronunciation Guide

ă p**a**t; oi b**oy**; ô p**aw**; th **th**in; ā p**ay**; ĭ p**i**t; ou **ou**t; th **th**is; är c**are**; ī p**ie**; ŏŏ t**oo**k; hw **wh**ich; ä f**a**ther; îr p**ier**; ōō b**oo**t; zh vi**si**on; ĕ p**e**t; ŏ p**o**t; ŭ c**u**t; ə **a**bout, it**e**m; ē b**e**; ō t**oe**; ûr **ur**ge; ♦ regionalism
Stress marks: ′ (primary); ′ (secondary), as in **dictionary** (dĭk′ shə-nĕr′ē)

Homographs

More Practice

B. Homographs in Action

Read the following passage aloud. Circle the correct pronunciation of each bold-faced homograph and write its definition. Use context clues and a dictionary to help you.

> Our **object** in visiting the **desert** was to learn how animals and plants **live** there. Although it was sunny, the **wind** and blowing sand soon began to **affect** our vision. I had to **wind** a scarf around my nose and **mouth.** I tried to **object** to the conditions, but couldn't even **mouth** the words. I was so covered with grit that I felt like a **live** sand sculpture.

1. object (ŏb-jĕkt', ŏb' jĭkt) meaning: _____

2. desert (dĕz' ərt, dĭ-zûrt') meaning: _____

3. live (līv, lĭv) meaning: _____

4. wind (wīnd, wĭnd) meaning: _____

5. affect (ə-fĕkt', ăf' ĕkt') meaning: _____

6. wind (wīnd, wĭnd) meaning: _____

7. mouth (mouth, mou*th*) meaning: _____

8. object (ŏb-jĕkt', ŏb' jĭkt) meaning: _____

9. mouth (mouth, mou*th*) meaning: _____

10. live (līv, lĭv) meaning: _____

C. Vocabulary Challenge

Each item below contains a homograph in bold-faced type. Determine the correct way to pronounce each one. (Use a dictionary if needed.) Then write a word or phrase that rhymes with the homograph.

> **EXAMPLE**   If you want to grow a garden this year, you will need to **sow** seeds in the next few weeks.
> rhyming word: *go*

1. Joe **wound** the hands of his wristwatch.

   Rhyming word: _____

2. How can you **refuse** that generous offer?

   Rhyming word: _____

3. I'm really angry, so don't **incense** me more.

   Rhyming word: _____

4. The magic of a sunset can totally **entrance** me.

   Rhyming word: _____

5. Your license expired a month ago and is now **invalid.**

   Rhyming word: _____

Lesson 31

Analogies

Teaching

Like similes and metaphors, **analogies** are comparisons. An analogy shows how two groups of words are related. Both groups of words are related in the same way. An analogy can be stated either using symbols or as a sentence.

Boring is to *dull* as *big* is to *large*.

BORING : DULL :: big : large

Means "is to" Means "as"

Gentle is to *harsh* as *friend* is to *enemy*.

GENTLE : HARSH :: friend: enemy

First group set in capital letters Second group set in small letters

Analogies can express several types of relationships between words.

Relationship	Example
Part to whole (A is part of B)	LEAF : TREE
Synonym (A means the same as B)	BORING : DULL
Antonym (A is the opposite of B)	GENTLE : HARSH
Item to category (A is an example of B)	POODLE : DOG
Worker to tool (A works with B)	FARMER : PLOW
Grammar (A is grammatically related to B)	RUN : RAN

A. Identifying Analogies

spoke	*pants*	*sculptor*	*do*	*ideal*
beverage	*fascinating*	*wrong*	*burner*	*sad*

Write the word from the list above that best completes each analogy. Then write the relationship expressed in the analogy. Use the chart to help you. You may also use a dictionary if needed.

EXAMPLE   COOKIES : DESSERT :: *chair* : furniture
relationship: *item to category*

1. FINGER : HAND :: _____ : wheel

   relationship: _____

2. IS : ARE :: does : _____

   relationship: _____

3. JOYFUL : UNHAPPY :: glad : _____

   relationship: _____

4. ARTIST: PAINT :: _____ : clay

   relationship: _____

5. CARROT : VEGETABLE :: tea : _____

   relationship: _____

6. BLADE : SKATE :: _____ : stove

   relationship: _____

7. SLEEPY : TIRED :: incorrect :

   relationship: _____

8. PATRIOT : PATRIOTISM :: _____ idealism

   relationship: _____

9. SNEAKER : SHOE :: jeans : _____

   relationship: _____

10. SIMPLE : COMPLEX :: boring : _____

   relationship: _____

Lesson 31

Analogies

More Practice

B. Analogies in Action

Circle the word in parentheses that best completes each analogy. Then write the type of relationship the analogy expresses. Use the chart on the previous page to help you. You may also use a dictionary if needed.

EXAMPLE LOUD : NOISY :: (awful, beautiful, attraction) : attractive
relationship: *synonym*

1. PLUMBER : WRENCH :: painter : (brush, easel, landscape)

   relationship: _____

2. GORILLA : MAMMAL :: (dolphin, salmon, turtle) : fish

   relationship: _____

3. TEACH : (LEARN, TAUGHT, TEACHER) :: skate: skater

   relationship: _____

4. (FAN, SOCCER, BALL) : SPORT :: tangerine: fruit

   relationship: _____

5. HUNGRY : FULL :: sleepy (snoring, energetic, lazy)

   relationship: _____

6. (FLIGHT, NEST, FEATHER) : BIRD :: scale : fish

   relationship: _____

7. ANGER : EMOTION :: (lamb, vegetable, food) : meat

   relationship: _____

8. TENNIS PLAYER : (BALL, NET, RACKET) :: baseball player: bat

   relationship: _____

9. BASHFUL : SHY :: jump : (jumpy, leap, timid)

   relationship: _____

10. ANKLE : (KNEE, WRIST, LEG) :: wrist : arm

    relationship: _____

C. Vocabulary Challenge

Complete each analogy and indicate the relationship it expresses. Use the chart on the previous page to help you. You may also use a dictionary if needed.

EXAMPLE SWIM : SWAM :: *study* : studied relationship: *grammar*

1. LATE : _____ :: anxious : nervous   relationship: _____

2. KIND : KINDEST :: _____ : fastest   relationship: _____

3. HAMMER : TOOL :: lily : _____   relationship: _____

Lesson 32

Using Your Strategies

Teaching

You have learned several basic strategies for figuring out a word's meaning:

- using the dictionary
- using context clues (general, restatement, definition, comparison, contrast, example)
- analyzing word parts (bases, roots, affixes)
- considering the meaning of related words.

Using a dictionary to learn the meaning of a new word is a good strategy for building your vocabulary. However, looking up a word means interrupting your reading. The other three strategies—using context clues, analyzing word parts, and learning from related words—can help you predict the meanings of new words *while* you read. You can look up the definitions later if you still need help.

A. Vocabulary Strategies in Action: Fiction

In the paragraphs below, use one or more of the vocabulary strategies you have learned to figure out the meaning of each underlined word. Then circle the strategy you used.

By the time the school spelling contest began, Abby was feeling <u>nauseated</u>. Her stomach was doing flip-flops, her palms were sweaty, and she couldn't sit still. She had <u>anticipated</u> this moment for so many days. Now, at last, what she'd looked forward to was finally happening.

She told herself that she had to calm down. She tried the breathing exercises her mother had taught her. She breathed in slowly, held her breath for a few seconds, then <u>exhaled</u> through her nose. She felt better.

Abby worried that she would <u>misspell</u> an easy word and feel embarrassed. However, as the spelling bee progressed, Abby felt increasingly encouraged. She hadn't misspelled a single word and there were fewer and fewer students left to compete with. Imagine her surprise when she was the only speller left at the end of the contest. The thunderous applause was <u>gratifying</u> to Abby. Even days later, she was thrilled by her achievement.

1. nauseated   meaning: _____
   strategy: context clues   word parts   related word   dictionary

2. anticipated   meaning: _____
   strategy: context clues   word parts   related word   dictionary

3. exhaled   meaning: _____
   strategy: context clues   word parts   related word   dictionary

4. misspell   meaning: _____
   strategy: context clues   word parts   related word   dictionary

5. gratifying   meaning: _____
   strategy: context clues   word parts   related word   dictionary

Using Your Strategies

Lesson 32

B. Vocabulary Strategies in Action: Nonfiction

In the paragraph below, use one of the vocabulary strategies you have learned to figure out the meaning of each underlined word. Then circle the strategy you used.

No one has lived in the Italian city of Pompeii for nearly 2,000 years. Yet thousands of tourists travel from distant places to visit it. These apparently <u>contradictory</u> facts can be explained by what happened in the summer of the year A.D. 79. In that year Mount Vesuvius, a huge mountain rising behind the city, exploded and <u>spewed</u> tons of hot volcanic ash on the city. Before the explosion, Pompeii was a <u>prosperous</u> city of 25,000 people. When the <u>eruption</u> ended, Pompeii was a dead city, <u>shrouded</u>, or buried, in volcanic ash.

Pompeii was finally discovered 1,500 years later. Everything under the layer of ash had remained <u>intact</u>—just as it had been on the day of the explosion. Today, Pompeii shows us what a city of the Roman Empire was like, down to the smallest detail.

1. contradictory   meaning: _____
   strategy: context clues   word parts   related word   dictionary

2. spewed   meaning: _____
   strategy: context clues   word parts   related word   dictionary

3. prosperous   meaning: _____
   strategy: context clues   word parts   related word   dictionary

4. eruption   meaning: _____
   strategy: context clues   word parts   related word   dictionary

5. shrouded   meaning: _____
   strategy: context clues   word parts   related word   dictionary

6. intact   meaning: _____
   strategy: context clues   word parts   related word   dictionary

C. Using Vocabulary Strategies

Write a paragraph using the words listed below. Apply the vocabulary strategies you have learned when you create your sentences so that a classmate would have to use these strategies to understand the four words.

foresight   *incredible*   *satisfactory*   *contradiction*

Personal Word List

Use the space below and on the next pages to create a list of words you want to
learn. Write the definition for each word and use it in a sentence to make sure you
make the word your own.

_____

_____

_____

_____

_____

_____

_____

_____

_____

_____

_____

_____

_____

_____

_____

_____

_____

_____

_____

_____

_____

_____

_____

Personal Word List (continued)

_____

_____

_____

_____

_____

_____

_____

_____

_____

_____

_____

_____

_____

_____

_____

_____

_____

_____

_____

_____

_____

_____

_____

Personal Word List (continued)

_____

_____

_____

_____

_____

_____

_____

_____

_____

_____

_____

_____

_____

_____

_____

_____

_____

_____

_____

_____

_____

_____

Personal Word List (continued)

_____

_____

_____

_____

_____

_____

_____

_____

_____

_____

_____

_____

_____

_____

_____

_____

_____

_____

_____

_____

_____

_____

Academic Vocabulary

Academic Vocabulary Lessons

Academic Vocabulary

Academic Words—History

Lesson 1

Academic Vocabulary

agriculture *n.* farming.

archaeological *adj.* having to do with the remains of ancient human life. [Greek: the root *archaeo,* from *arkhaio,* ancient, and the suffixes *-logy*, study of, *-ic*, like, and *-al,* relating to.]

architecture *n.* the art and science of designing and creating buildings; the style of buildings.

commerce *n.* the buying and selling of goods; business and trade.

community *n.* a group of people living in the same place or with common or similar interests.

culture *n.* human activities and thought such as art, literature, religion, and politics.

domestication *n.* training animals or plants to be useful to humans. [Latin: root *domus,* home, and the suffixes *-ic,* like, *-ate*, to cause, and *-ion,* act of.]

metallurgy *n.* the study of the properties and uses of metals.

Break It Down—domestication

root	suffix	suffix	suffix
word part ➤ **domus**		**ate**	
meaning ➤	like		act of

A. Match each word with its definition. Write the letter of the matching word in the blank.

_____ 1. a group of people living together

_____ 2. the art and science of building

_____ 3. the study of metals

_____ 4. the buying and selling of goods

_____ 5. having to do with the study of ancient human objects

A. archaeological

B. architecture

C. commerce

D. community

E. metallurgy

B. Write the letter of the word or phrase that best completes each sentence.

_____ 1. You would expect someone interested in **architecture** to study
a) animals.   b) farming.   c) buildings.

_____ 2. People in a **community** are
a) far apart.   b) connected to each other.   c) old.

_____ 3. The **domestication** of animals involves
a) taming and training them.   b) painting them.   c) acting like them.

_____ 4. The **culture** of a group of people includes its
a) mountains, rivers, and lakes.   b) weather.   c) art, science, and government.

Lesson 2

Academic Words—History

Academic Vocabulary

caste *n.* a social class, especially in Hindu society.

civic *adj.* having to do with a city or its citizens. [Latin: word *civicus,* from *civis,* citizen.]

economy *n.* the system dealing with the activity of money, materials, and labor.

ethical *adj.* relating to right behavior; good values. [Greek: root *ethos,* character, and the suffixes –*ic,* like, and –*al,* relating to.]

monotheistic *adj.* believing that there is one god. [Greek: prefix *mono-,* one, the root *theos,* god, and the suffixes –*ist,* one who believes, and -*ic,* like.]

mythology *n.* the collection of stories a culture tells to explain its origin, history, gods, and heroes; folk tales and legends. [Greek: root *muthos,* story, and suffix –*logy,* study of.]

philosophy *n.* the study of what people believe and how they should act; a system of values that a person decides to live by.

social *adj.* related to living together in groups; having to do with humans and the ways they decide to organize.

Break It Down—monotheistic

prefix	root	suffix	suffix
word part	**theos**		**ic**
meaning one		believer	

A. Write the letter of the vocabulary word that best completes each sentence.

_____ 1. Animals that live together in groups are _____ beings.
a) monotheistic b) social c) civic

_____ 2. _____ is the study of ancient stories about the world.
a) Economy b) Philosophy c) Mythology

_____ 3. If you want to learn about a country's money and materials, study its
a) mythology. b) caste. c) economy.

_____ 4. People who believe in one god are
a) monotheistic. b) ethical. c) social.

_____ 5. Ideas that deal with right behavior are
a) civic. b) social. c) ethical.

_____ 6. The study of how people know and should act is
a) mythology. b) philosophy. c) economy.

_____ 7. Matters that have to do with a city and its residents are
a) ethical. b) civic. c) monotheistic.

_____ 8. A person's class in society is his or her
a) economy. b) philosophy. c) caste.

B. Read the paragraph first. Then fill in each blank with the correct vocabulary word.

ethical   philosophy   monotheistic   social

Some people think that _____ is an important subject to study because it deals with human knowledge and action. One branch of that field has to do with right, or _____ behavior. People can find answers there for many _____ problems of living in a community. This is true if the people are _____ , or if they believe in many gods or in no god at all.

Academic Words—History

Academic Vocabulary

citizen *n.* a person living in a country, state, or city who is entitled to its rights and subject to its laws.

democratic *adj.* characterized by government by the people; the decisions for the country are made through the people's right to voting of some type.

dictatorship *n.* a government under the rule of a single leader or group of people; a system run by an all-powerful leader. [Latin: root *dictare*, to say, and the suffixes

-ate, to cause, *–or*, one who, and *–ship*, condition of.]

justice *n.* fairness; upholding laws.

political *adj.* having to do with the matters of government or the state.

republic *n.* a country or state that is usually ruled by a president in modern times and whose citizens vote for its lawmakers; a form of government where the people have representation. (Latin: prefix *re-*, to give, and root *publica*, of the people.)

Break It Down—dictatorship

root	suffix	suffix	suffix
dictare			**ship**
	to cause	one who	

word part / *meaning*

A. Match each word with its definition. Write the letter of the matching word in the blank.

a. *citizen*   b. *democratic*   c. *dictatorship*   d. *justice*   e. *political*   f. *republic*

_____ 1. characterized by government by the people

_____ 2. having to do with the affairs of government

_____ 3. fairness

_____ 4. a country usually ruled by a president with participation by citizens

_____ 5. the resident of a country or state

_____ 6. a government under the rule of an all-powerful person

B. Write the letter of the word or phrase that best completes each sentence.

_____ 1. If you were interested in **political** matters, you might study about
a) literature.
b) government and laws.
c) medicine.

_____ 2. People living in a **democratic** country have
a) no more than one child.
b) a king or queen.
c) the right to vote.

_____ 3. Treating other people with **justice** means
a) being fair.
b) making them wait in line.
c) making them get a license before they can drive.

_____ 4. If you lived in a **dictatorship,** you probably
a) wouldn't be able to vote for the leader of your choice.
b) would have an easy life.
c) would have all the freedom you wanted.

_____ 5. Being a **citizen** of a country entitles you to
a) a computer.
b) protection under its laws.
c) a birth certificate.

_____ 6. People living in a **republic** have
a) a religious leader.
b) a king.
c) representation in their country's government.

Lesson 4 # Academic Words—History

ago *adv., adj.* gone by; past; meaning in the past.

century *n.* one hundred years. [Latin: root *centum*, hundred, and the suffix *-ry*, collection of.]

era *n.* a particular time from one date to another; historical age.

fall *v.* to drop down; descend.

period *n.* an interval of time; term.

rise *v.* to move up; ascend.

Break It Down—century

root	suffix
centum	
	collection of

word part → centum →

meaning →

A. Match each word with its synonym. Write the letter of the matching word in the blank.

_____ 1. historical age   A. ago

_____ 2. ascend   B. century

_____ 3. 100 years   C. era

_____ 4. past   D. fall

_____ 5. interval of time   E. period

_____ 6. descend   F. rise

B. Fill in each blank in the paragraph with the correct vocabulary word.

    ago   century   era

    fall   period   rise

In history, we study events that happened years _____. The

_____ between the years 1800 and 1900, for example, is very

interesting to study. This interval of time is also called the 19th _____.

People who lived in this _____ saw industry _____, or become

more successful. As a result, these people also saw farming _____, or

decline.

Lesson 5 # Academic Words—Math   *Academic Vocabulary*

decimals *n.* numbers smaller than a whole number expressed with a decimal point; a way of writing fractions with a denominator that is a power of ten. *The number 0.67 is a decimal.*

denominator *n.* the bottom number of a fraction that tells how many parts the fraction is divided into. [Latin: prefix *de-,* from, the root *nominare,* to name, and the suffixes *-ate,* to cause, and *-or,* one that.]

fractions *n.* numbers represented as the division of one number by another. *The number* $\frac{2}{3}$ *is a fraction.*

percent *n.* a part of a whole expressed in hundredths, as 66%; another way of writing a fraction with a denominator of 100. [Latin: prefix *per-,* for each, and root *centum,* hundred.]

rate *n.* a quantity of something measured per unit of something else, as 55 miles/ hour; expressed by division.

ratio *n.* the relationship between two numbers. *The ratio of apples to oranges is 1:2.*

Break It Down—denominator

prefix	root	suffix	suffix
word part	**nominare**	**ate**	
meaning from			one that

A. Match each word with its example. Write the letter of the matching word in the blank.

_____ 1. 37%

_____ 2. 588 dots/square inch

_____ 3. 4:7

_____ 4. 0.26341, 0.008

_____ 5. $\frac{5}{9}$, $\frac{1}{3}$

_____ 6. the number 3, in $\frac{1}{3}$

A. decimals

B. denominator

C. fractions

D. percent

E. rate

F. ratio

B. Write **T** if the sentence is true and **F** if it is false.

_____ 1. A **fraction,** a **percent,** a **rate,** and a **ratio** all express the result of one number divided by another or the relationship of one number to another.

_____ 2. Another way of expressing **fractions** is to write them as **decimals.**

_____ 3. The **denominator** of a **fraction** is the number on top.

_____ 4. One way to write a **rate** is 3:5.

_____ 5. The **percent** 50% is equal to the **fraction** $\frac{1}{2}$.

_____ 6. 100 miles/hour is not a **rate.**

_____ 7. 6:7 is not a **ratio.**

_____ 8. **Fractions** are represented as the multiplication of two numbers.

Lesson 6 # Academic Words—Math

constant *n.* a number that has a value that never changes such as {1, 2, 3, 4 etc.}.

equation *n.* a statement that two mathematical expressions are equal, as x −7 = 34. [Latin: root *aequus*, level, equal, and the suffixes -*ate*, to cause, and -*ion*, result of.]

factor *n.* a number in a mathematical expression that is multiplied or divided by another number.

integer *n.* any positive or negative whole number or zero such as {-2,-1, 0, 1, 2}.

negative *adj.* a number that is less than zero.

positive *adj.* a number that is more than zero.

Break It Down—equation

root	suffix	suffix
word part aequus	>	> ion
meaning level	to cause	

A. Write the letter of the vocabulary word that best completes each sentence.

_____ 1. A number that is more than zero is
a) positive.
b) negative.
c) an integer.

_____ 2. The expression 6x + 3 = 15 is an example of
a) an integer.
b) a constant.
c) an equation.

_____ 3. In the expression 6x + 3 = 15, the number 3 is
a) a constant.
b) an equation.
c) negative.

_____ 4. In the expression 6x + 3 = 15, 6 and x are both
a) negative.
b) factors.
c) unknown.

_____ 5. A number that you cannot show by counting on your fingers is
a) positive.
b) a factor.
c) negative.

_____ 6. Each of the numbers 254, −67, 0, and 1 is
a) an integer.
b) positive.
c) an equation.

B. Match each word with its example. Write the letter of the matching word in the blank.

_____ 1. 8 or 7 in the number 56 (remember 8 multiplied by 7 is equal to 56)

_____ 2. -0.25, -64

_____ 3. 4, 0, -79

_____ 4. 55, 6.93, 145.86

_____ 5. 4x + 2 = 10

_____ 6. 35 in the expression x - 35 = 155

A. constant
B. equation
C. factor
D. integer
E. negative
F. positive

Lesson
7
Academic Words—Math

Academic Vocabulary

adjacent *adj.* next to, close to, or lying near.

circumference *n.* the distance; or measurement around a circle. [Latin: prefix *circum,* around, and root *ferre,* to carry, and the suffix *-ence,* process.]

complementary *adj.* two angles that total 90 degrees.

isosceles *adj.* a triangle that has two equal sides. [Greek: prefix *iso-,* same, and root *skelos,* leg.]

parallel *adj.* two or more lines that are straight and will never intersect; the same distance apart everywhere and never meeting. [Latin: prefix *para-,* beside, and root *allelon,* of one another.]

perimeter *n.* the distance around something. [Greek: prefix *peri-,* around, and root *metron,* measure.]

perpendicular *adj.* when two lines meet at 90° to one another, at a right angle.

polygon *n.* a figure having many sides and angles. [Greek: prefix *poly-,* many, and root *gonia,* angle.]

Break It Down—circumference

prefix	root	suffix
word part	**ferre**	
meaning	around	process

A. Write the letter of the word or phrase that best completes each sentence.

_____ 1. A **polygon**
    a) has many sides and angles.
    b) has two parallel lines.
    c) is a circle.

_____ 2. The **circumference** of a circle is
    a) the distance around it.
    b) the length of a line perpendicular to it.
    c) the distance to a line parallel to it.

_____ 3. The **adjacent** sides of a figure are the sides
    a) opposite to each other.
    b) of the same length.
    c) next to each other.

_____ 4. **Parallel** lines
    a) cross each other twice.
    b) form a right, 90 degree angle.
    c) never meet.

_____ 5. **Complementary** angles
    a) are parallel.
    b) total 90 degrees.
    c) total 180 degrees.

_____ 6. Lines that are **perpendicular**
    a) are at a 90-degree angle.
    b) are parallel.
    c) are a polygon.

B. Write **T** if the sentence is true and **F** if it is false.

_____ 1. **Parallel** lines form **complementary** angles.

_____ 2. The **circumference** of a circle is its **perimeter.**

_____ 3. An **isosceles** triangle is a kind of polygon.

_____ 4. **Perpendicular** lines are **adjacent.**

Academic Words—Math

Lesson 8

equal *adj.* the same.

greater than *adj.* more or larger in number.

less than *adj.* fewer or smaller in number.

minus *adj.* made smaller by, taken away from.

multiply *v.* to find the product by multiplication; times. [Latin: prefix *multi-*, many, and root *plex*, fold, and the suffix *–y*, performing.]

plus *adj.* made larger by, added to.

Break It Down—multiply

prefix	root	verb suffix
multi		
	fold	performing

word part ▶

meaning ▶

A. Match each word with its synonym. Write the letter of the matching word in the blank.

_____ 1. times

_____ 2. added to

_____ 3. fewer

_____ 4. the same

_____ 5. more

_____ 6. taken away from

A. equal

B. greater than

C. less than

D. minus

E. multiply

F. plus

B. Write the letter of the word or phrase that best completes each sentence.

_____ 1. If two things are **equal,**
    a) the first one is greater than the second.
    b) the first one is less than the second.
    c) they are the same.

_____ 2. The answer to the problem 15 **minus** 9 is
    a) less than 15.
    b) greater than 15.
    c) equal to 15.

_____ 3. The answer to the problem 15 **plus** 9 is
    a) equal to 15 minus 9.
    b) greater than 15 minus 9.
    c) equal to 26.

_____ 4. If you **multiply** two positive numbers together, the answer is
    a) equal to one number plus the other.
    b) greater than one number plus the other.
    c) equal to the larger number minus the smaller number.

_____ 5. The word or phrase whose meaning is closest to **plus** is
    a) less than.
    b) multiply
    c) equal

_____ 6. The answer to the problem 21 **plus** 3 is _____ the answer to the problem 21 minus 3.
    a) greater than
    b) equal to
    c) not

Academic Words—Science

Academic Vocabulary

atmosphere *n.* the mass of air surrounding the earth. [Greek root *atmos-*, vapor, and the Latin root *sphaera,* ball.]

climate *n.* the average weather conditions over time of an area, including temperature, wind, amount of snow, and rain; the particular conditions of one area.

condensation *n.* the process by which a gas or vapor changes to a liquid.

hurricane *n.* a severe tropical cyclone (a violent rotating windstorm) beginning near the equator and usually involving heavy rains.

precipitation *n.* any form of water, such as rain or snow, that falls to the earth's surface.

tornado *n.* a rotating column of air whirling at high speeds and usually accompanied by a funnel-shaped downward extension of a cloud.

Break It Down—atmosphere

Greek root	Latin root
word part ▶	▷ **sphaera**
meaning ▶ vapor	

A. Match each word with its definition. Write the letter of the matching word in the blank.

_____ 1. a rotating column of air whirling at high speeds

_____ 2. rain or snow

_____ 3. the mass of air surrounding the earth

_____ 4. the process of gas changing to liquid

_____ 5. a severe tropical storm usually involving violent winds and heavy rains

_____ 6. the average weather conditions over time of an area

A. climate

B. condensation

C. tornado

D. atmosphere

E. hurricane

F. precipitation

B. Write **T** if the sentence is true and **F** if the sentence is false.

_____ 1. A **hurricane** is usually accompanied by a funnel-shaped downward extension of a cloud.

_____ 2. **Precipitation** is water that falls to the earth.

_____ 3. The **atmosphere** is all of the water on the earth.

_____ 4. **Condensation** is when liquid turns to gas.

_____ 5. The **climate** includes the temperature, wind, amount of snow, and rain for a given region.

_____ 6. A **tornado** can be very destructive.

Academic Words—Science

Academic Vocabulary

core *n.* the central part of the earth where the inner part is solid and the outer part is liquid.

crust *n.* the outer part of the surface of the earth.

deposit *v.* to lay down.

dynamic *adj.* something that has continuous change. [Greek: root *dynamis-*, power, and the suffix *-ic*, like.]

erode *v.* to wear away.

mantle *n.* the part of the earth that lies between the crust and the core.

Break It Down—dynamic

root	suffix
word part dynamis	
meaning	like

A. Write the letter of the word or phrase that best completes each sentence.

_____ 1. The **core** of the earth lies
    a) on the earth's surface.
    b) at its center.
    c) under water.

_____ 2. In a **dynamic** process,
    a) nothing ever changes.
    b) things change all the time.
    c) dynamite creates an explosion.

_____ 3. The **mantle** of the earth lies
    a) between the crust and the core.
    b) on the surface of the earth.
    c) within the core.

_____ 4. For something to **erode,** it must
    a) grow larger.
    b) be in the earth's mantle.
    c) wear away.

_____ 5. When water and wind **deposit** pieces of rock and sand in a river,
    a) they take this material away.
    b) they lay this material down.
    c) they are not being dynamic.

_____ 6. The **crust** of the earth is
    a) under the mantle.
    b) at the surface.
    c) inside the core.

B. Write **T** if a sentence is true and **F** if it is false.

_____ 1. Another word for the earth's core is **mantle.**

_____ 2. The fact that the earth is constantly changing means that it is a **dynamic** planet.

_____ 3. **Deposit** and **erode** are opposite actions.

_____ 4. To get to the surface of the earth from its center, you don't have to pass through the **mantle.**

_____ 5. To get to the **mantle** of the earth from the surface, you have to pass through the **crust.**

_____ 6. The forces like wind and water **deposit** material on the earth.

Academic Words—Science

Academic Vocabulary

biomes *n.* a geographic region or area with a very specific plant life and climate such as a desert or rain forest.

ecology *n.* the science that deals with the relationship between organisms, such as plants and animals, and their environment. [Greek: root *oikos*, house, and suffix *-logy*, study of.]

ecosystem *n.* an environment functioning as a unit such as a pond.

organism *n.* a living thing.

renewable *adj.* able to be replaced through natural processes or by good human care. [Greek: prefix *re-*, again, and root *neos*, new, and the suffix *-able*, capable of.]

resource *n.* the supply of a natural material, such as water or oil.

Break It Down—ecology

	root	suffix
word part		**logy**
meaning	house	

A. Write the letter of the vocabulary word that best completes each sentence.

_____ 1. Something that can be replaced is
  a) an ecosystem.
  b) an organism.
  c) renewable.

_____ 2. A natural supply of a useful material such as water is known as
  a) a resource.
  b) an ecosystem.
  c) an organism.

_____ 3. A living being is called
  a) a resource.
  b) an organism.
  c) ecology.

_____ 4. Specific living communities are called
  a) renewable.
  b) a resource.
  c) biomes.

_____ 5. The study of the relationship of organisms and their environments is
  a) ecology.
  b) renewable.
  c) a resource.

_____ 6. Organisms and their environment functioning as a unit are known as
  a) a resource.
  b) renewable.
  c) an ecosystem.

B. Fill in each blank in the paragraph with the correct vocabulary word.

biomes   ecology   ecosystem   organism   renewable   resource

If you are going to do your part to keep the earth alive and healthy, you should learn all you can about the science of _____. That knowledge will make you aware of the many _____ that make up the earth's variety of living communities. It will help you understand how human activities are using up one _____ after another and that many of these precious materials are not _____. Once they are gone, they're gone for good. You will come to appreciate the delicate balance in an _____ between an _____, or living thing, and the environment that supports it.

Academic Words—Science

Academic Vocabulary

cause *n.* the reason something happens.

effect *n.* something brought about by a cause; a result.

experiment *n.* a test done to prove how or why something happens; *v.* to conduct such a test. [Latin: root *experiri*, to test, and the suffix *-ment*, result.]

hypothesis *n.* an idea about how something happens that still needs to be tested by an experiment. [Greek: prefix *hypo-*, under, and root *tithenai*, to place.]

result *n.*, a consequence or effect; *v.* to occur as a consequence.

variable *n.* something that can change its value, the opposite of a constant; *adv.* subject to change, not constant.

Break It Down—experiment

	root	suffix
word part	experiri	
meaning		result

A. Match each word with the statement that describes it. Write the letter of the matching word in the blank.

_____ 1. Do this to test why something happens.   A. cause

_____ 2. This produces an effect.   B. effect

_____ 3. Do an experiment to test if this is correct.   C. experiment

_____ 4. This can take on different values.   D. hypothesis

_____ 5. An effect is the same as this.   E. result

_____ 6. This is the result of a cause.   F. variable

B. Choose the correct word and part from the parentheses to correctly complete each sentence.

1. **experiment (verb) / experiment (noun)**

   You have to _____ to see if your theory is true.

   In performing your _____, it is best to keep as many factors as you can constant and just have one variable.

2. **result (verb) / result (noun)**

   That way, it will be easier to explain whatever may _____.

   It's more likely, though, that you will have to do the process again to see if the _____ is the same or variable.

Spelling

Spelling Lessons

Lesson 1 · Silent *e* words and suffixes

Teaching

require ⟶ requiring   requi<u>re</u>s   requi<u>re</u>ment
achieve ⟶ achieving   achie<u>ve</u>s   achie<u>ve</u>ment
provide ⟶ providing   provi<u>de</u>s
separate ⟶ separating   separa<u>te</u>s   separa<u>te</u>ly
pursue ⟶ pursuing   pursu<u>e</u>s
complete ⟶ completing   comple<u>te</u>s   comple<u>te</u>ly
imagine ⟶ imagining   imagin<u>e</u>s
introduce ⟶ introducing   introdu<u>ce</u>s
continue ⟶ continuing   continu<u>e</u>s

Lesson Generalization: A **suffix** is a word ending that changes the use of a word. To add a suffix to a word that ends with a final silent **e**, drop the **e** if the suffix begins with a vowel. Keep the **e** if the suffix begins with a consonant.

pursuing   completely

A. Complete the following exercise.

1. When **ing** is added to words ending in a silent **e**, what happens to the **e**?

_____

Write those words ending in **ing**.

_____   _____   _____

_____   _____   _____

_____   _____   _____

2. When **s, ment,** and **ly** were added to the words ending in silent **e**, what happened to the **e**?

_____

Write the words ending in **s, ment,** and **ly.**

_____   _____   _____

_____   _____   _____

_____   _____   _____

_____   _____   _____

_____

B. Read the word list again. Note the spelling of each word. Then, on a separate sheet of paper, use each word with a suffix in an original sentence.

Name _____ Date _____

 Lesson 1

Silent *e* words and suffixes

More Practice

1. requiring	9. separating	17. imagining
2. requires	10. separates	18. imagines
3. requirement	11. separately	19. introducing
4. achieving	12. pursuing	20. introduces
5. achieves	13. pursues	21. continuing
6. achievement	14. completing	22. continues
7. providing	15. completes	
8. provides	16. completely	

A. Complete each pair of sentences with two forms of the underlined word.

1. <u>separate</u> Let's wrap each gift _____.

   Miguel is _____ the puzzle into pieces.

2. <u>require</u> Past experience is one _____ for the job.

   The coach will be _____ more practice time.

3. <u>pursue</u> The police were _____ the speeding car.

   Our art teacher _____ her own art projects.

4. <u>complete</u> Marcia never _____ her work early.

   The paint is not _____ dry yet.

5. <u>achieve</u> Climbing that mountain would be a great _____.

   Mark _____ every goal he sets for himself.

6. <u>introduce</u> Carol keeps _____ me to her friends.

   Walk on stage after the speaker _____ you.

7. <u>continue</u> The program _____ after the intermission.

   The baby was _____ to cry.

8. <u>provide</u> A local store is _____ uniforms for the team.

   That tree _____ us with apples every autumn.

9. <u>imagine</u> My brother _____ he sees pictures in the clouds.

   I keep _____ I hear footsteps downstairs.

B. On a separate sheet of paper, write the **ing** form of the spelling words in alphabetical order. Then write the **s** form of each word.

Lesson 2

The suffix *ance*

Teaching

clear + ance = clear<u>ance</u>	inherit + ance = inherit<u>ance</u>
perform + ance = perform<u>ance</u>	annoy + ance = annoy<u>ance</u>
disturb + ance = disturb<u>ance</u>	avoid + ance = avoid<u>ance</u>
allow + ance = allow<u>ance</u>	resemble + ance = resembl<u>ance</u>
accept + ance = accept<u>ance</u>	insure + ance = insur<u>ance</u>
attend + ance = attend<u>ance</u>	endure + ance = endur<u>ance</u>
assist + ance = assist<u>ance</u>	assure + ance = assur<u>ance</u>
appear + ance = appear<u>ance</u>	observe + ance = observ<u>ance</u>
acquaint + ance = acquaint<u>ance</u>	guide + ance = guid<u>ance</u>

Lesson Generalization: The suffix **ance** is commonly added to complete words to form nouns or adjectives.

Her <u>resemblance</u> to her sister was amazing.

He made an <u>acceptance</u> speech.

A. Compete the following exercises.

1. Look for base words in the word list that end in silent **e**. When the suffix **ance** is added to

    those words, what happens to the final **e** of the base word? _____

    Write the spelling words that are created when **ance** is added to a base word with a final silent **e**.

    _____   _____   _____

    _____   _____   _____

2. What happens when **ance** is added to base words that do not end in a silent **e**?

    _____

    Write those spelling words that are created when **ance** is added to a base word that does

    not end in a silent **e**.

    _____   _____   _____

    _____   _____   _____

    _____   _____   _____

    _____   _____   _____

B. On a separate sheet of paper, use each spelling word in a sentence. Then rewrite
the sentences, leaving a blank for the spelling words. Arrange your sentences in an
order that does not match the order the spelling words are presented in the list. Then
trade papers with a partner and try to fill in the blanks.

Lesson 2

The suffix *ance*

More Practice

1. clearance	7. assistance	13. resemblance
2. performance	8. appearance	14. insurance
3. allowance	9. acquaintance	15. endurance
4. disturbance	10. inheritance	16. assurance
5. acceptance	11. annoyance	17. observance
6. attendance	12. avoidance	18. guidance

A. Complete each sentence with a word from the spelling list.

1. Mark spent his _____ to buy a football.

2. The actor gave a good _____ in tonight's play.

3. The department store had a _____ sale on summer clothing.

4. All of the concert's organizers expected _____ to be excellent.

5. The two workers needed _____ in moving the huge crate.

6. The dog created a _____ when it ran into the store.

7. Fraternal twins may show little _____ to each other.

8. The governor made a brief _____ at the state fair.

9. Is Myra a good friend or only an _____ ?

10. Race car drivers need good accident _____ .

11. The newly elected class president prepared an _____ speech.

12. Competitive swimming requires great _____ .

13. The town's _____ of the Fourth of July included parades and fireworks.

14. Leon got everyone's _____ that they would be on time.

15. The will stated that each person was to receive an _____ of $1,000.

16. My aunt is a school _____ counselor.

17. The loud noise brought a look of _____ to Ann's face.

18. Some diets require the _____ of certain foods.

B. On a separate sheet of paper, create a word search puzzle using all of the words from the spelling list. Trade puzzles with a partner. Try to solve your partner's puzzle. Can you find all 18 words?

Plurals of words that end with *o*

Teaching

studio	+ s	= studios	banjo	+ s	= banjos		
radio	+ s	= radios	piano	+ s	= pianos		
rodeo	+ s	= rodeos	kangaroo	+ s	= kangaroos		
stereo	+ s	= stereos	zero	+ s	= zeros		
patio	+ s	= patios	lasso	+ s	= lassos		
ratio	+ s	= ratios	halo	+ s	= halos		
igloo	+ s	= igloos	silo	+ s	= silos		
echo	+ es	= echoes	potato	+ es	= potatoes		
hero	+ es	= heroes	tomato	+ es	= tomatoes		

Lesson Generalization: Singular means one. **Plural** means more than one. Most singular nouns are made plural by adding the letter **s**. Most nouns that end with the letter **o** are also made plural by adding the letter **s**. A few nouns that end with **o** are made plural by adding **es**.

A. Complete the following exercise.

1. Most singular nouns ending in **o** are made plural by adding

   _____. Write the plural forms of the words from the word list

   that follow this rule.

   _____   _____   _____

   _____   _____   _____

   _____   _____   _____

   _____   _____   _____

   _____   _____

2. A few nouns ending in **o** are an exception to the rule. These exceptions are made

   plural by adding _____. Write the plural forms of the words

   from the word list that are exceptions to the rule.

   _____   _____   _____

   _____

B. On a separate sheet of paper, write the plural forms of the words from the word list in alphabetical order. Check your list to make sure that you have added the correct plural endings.

Lesson 3

Plurals of words that end with *o*

1. studios	7. igloos	13. halos
2. radios	8. banjos	14. silos
3. rodeos	9. pianos	15. echoes
4. stereos	10. kangaroos	16. heroes
5. patios	11. zeros	17. potatoes
6. ratios	12. lassos	18. tomatoes

A. The words in each group are related in some way. Find words from the spelling list that fit into each group.

1. carrots, onions, _____ , _____

2. recorders, phonographs, _____ , _____

3. guitars, organs, _____ , _____

4. horses, cowboys, _____ , _____

5. huts, apartments, tepees, _____

6. decks, porches, terraces, _____

B. Write the plural form of the spelling word that matches each clue and fits in the puzzle.

Across

3. relation of one number to another

5. Australian animal

7. number

11. artist's work room

12. Western talent contest

Down

1. ring of light

2. ice house

4. paved area by a house

6. part of a barn

8. broadcasting device

9. repeated sound

10. record player

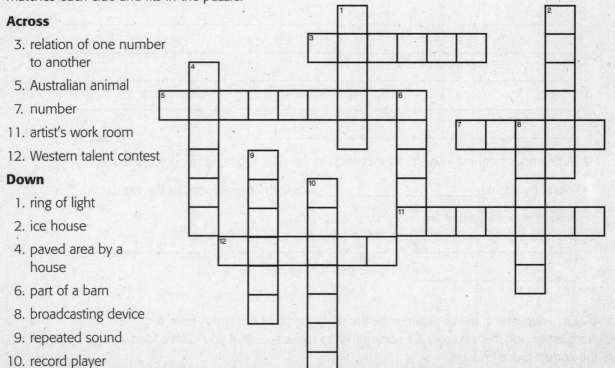

Prefixes and base words

Lesson 4

re + search = research	dis + courage = discourage	pre + caution = precaution
re + condition = recondition	dis + prove = disprove	pre + arrange = prearrange
re + fuel = refuel	dis + ability = disability	pre + diction = prediction
re + vision = revision	dis + agreement = disagreement	pre + mature = premature
re + elect = reelect	dis + advantage = disadvantage	pre + face = preface
re + surface = resurface	dis + regard = disregard	pre + school = preschool

Lesson Generalization: A **prefix** is a group of letters added to the beginning of a word to make a word with a different meaning. A prefix can be added directly to a complete word to make a new word. No change is made in the prefix or the base word.

A. Complete the following exercises.

1. Look at the words in the list above. Note that when a prefix is added to each base word, neither the prefix nor the base word changes spelling. What prefix is added to the words in the first column?

   _____ Write those words. Circle the prefix in each.

   _____ _____ _____

   _____ _____ _____

2. What prefix is added to the words in the second column? _____
   Write those words. Circle the prefix in each.

   _____ _____ _____

   _____ _____ _____

3. What prefix is added to the words in the third column? _____
   Write those words. Circle the prefix in each.

   _____ _____ _____

   _____ _____ _____

B. Mix and match prefixes and base words using only the words in the list. Try new combinations until you find real words, and write the words on a separate sheet of paper. Compare your list to a partner's list.

Prefixes and base words

More Practice

1. research	7. discourage	13. precaution
2. recondition	8. disprove	14. prearrange
3. refuel	9. disability	15. prediction
4. revision	10. disagreement	16. premature
5. reelect	11. disadvantage	17. preface
6. resurface	12. disregard	18. preschool

A. Add the missing vowels to complete each spelling word.

1. d __ s __ dv __ nt __ g __

2. pr __ c __ __ t __ __ n

3. pr __ __ rr __ ng __

4. d __ s __ gr __ __ m __ nt

5. d __ sr __ g __ rd

6. pr __ m __ t __ r __

7. d __ s __ b __ l __ ty

8. r __ s __ __ rch

9. r __ v __ s __ __ n

10. r __ f __ __ l

11. pr __ f __ c __

12. r __ s __ rf __ c __

B. Complete each sentence with a word from the spelling list.

1. Did the two boys have a _____ over who would be in charge?

2. Did your parents _____ your absence with the attendance office?

3. Rina had read only the _____ of the book.

4. Mark was doing _____ on sharks for his report.

5. The counselors took every _____ to make the camp safe for children.

6. The drivers must _____ their cars twice during the race.

7. Will losing the contest _____ Fran from trying again?

8. The announcement that school would close because of the snow was _____ .

9. Jim had been absent, so he was at a _____ when he took the test.

10. Will your little brother attend _____ this year?

11. Leon does not consider his injury to be a serious _____ .

12. This polish helps to _____ old leather.

13. Do you think the class will _____ the same officers?

14. We all made a _____ about who would win the World Series.

15. The scientist was unable to _____ the excellent research.

Prefixes and roots

Teaching

in + sist = in<u>sist</u>
con + sist = con<u>sist</u>

in + spire = in<u>spire</u>
con + spire = con<u>spire</u>

in + struct = in<u>struct</u>
con + struct = con<u>struct</u>

in + clude = in<u>clude</u>
con + clude = con<u>clude</u>

in + flict = in<u>flict</u>
con + flict = con<u>flict</u>

de + tain = de<u>tain</u>
re + tain = re<u>tain</u>

in + flate = in<u>flate</u>
de + flate = de<u>flate</u>

de + cline = de<u>cline</u>
re + cline = re<u>cline</u>

in + cis + ion = in<u>cis</u>ion
de + cis + ion = de<u>cis</u>ion

Lesson Generalization: Roots are word parts that cannot stand alone. They grow into words when they are joined to prefixes (added before roots) or suffixes (added after roots). A root can be joined with many different prefixes. Changing the prefix changes the meaning.

in (in, into) + **struct** (build) = **instruct**   <u>instruct</u> people

con (together, with) + **struct** (build) = **construct**   <u>construct</u> buildings

A. Complete the following exercises.

1. What four prefixes are added to the roots in the word list?

_____   _____   _____

_____

2. Nine roots are used in the words from the word list. Write each root and the two prefixes that have been added to that root.

Prefix	Prefix	Root
_____	_____	_____
_____	_____	_____
_____	_____	_____
_____	_____	_____
_____	_____	_____
_____	_____	_____
_____	_____	_____
_____	_____	_____
_____	_____	_____

B. On a separate sheet of paper, write the words from the spelling list with a brief definition for each.

Lesson 5

Prefixes and roots

1. insist	7. detain	13. include
2. consist	8. retain	14. conclude
3. instruct	9. decline	15. incision
4. construct	10. recline	16. decision
5. inflict	11. inspire	17. inflate
6. conflict	12. conspire	18. deflate

A. Unscramble the letters and write the spelling word. First, find the letters of the prefix. They are not scrambled.

1. tsinis _____
2. antrei _____
3. riconpes _____
4. elccondu _____
5. siinnoic _____
6. iclintf _____
7. rstcuint _____
8. tlconcfi _____
9. feldeat _____

10. siidenco _____
11. atdeni _____
12. stconsi _____
13. ledincu _____
14. creilne _____
15. tsurccont _____
16. prinesi _____
17. nildece _____
18. talfine _____

B. Write the word from the spelling list that is the synonym (means the same) or antonym (means the opposite) of each word below.

1. scheme (synonym) _____
2. begin (antonym) _____
3. cut (synonym) _____
4. demand (synonym) _____
5. destroy (antonym) _____
6. stand (antonym) _____
7. accord (synonym) _____
8. shrink (antonym) _____
9. hold (synonym) _____

10. teach (synonym) _____
11. discourage (antonym) _____
12. contain (synonym) _____
13. judgment (synonym) _____
14. inflate (antonym) _____
15. refuse (synonym) _____
16. impose (synonym) _____
17. peace (antonym) _____
18. comprise (synonym) _____

Words ending with *ary*

Teaching

tempor<u>ary</u>	compliment<u>ary</u>	diet<u>ary</u>
summ<u>ary</u>	extraordin<u>ary</u>	heredit<u>ary</u>
liter<u>ary</u>	honor<u>ary</u>	supplement<u>ary</u>
second<u>ary</u>	volunt<u>ary</u>	burgl<u>ary</u>
prim<u>ary</u>	contempor<u>ary</u>	itiner<u>ary</u>
prelimin<u>ary</u>	solit<u>ary</u>	necess<u>ary</u>

Lesson Generalization: The **ary** ending begins with a vowel that is indistinct. The **a** is difficult to tell from an **e** when it is followed by the letter **r**. The ending **ary** can sound almost like **ery** in **very**. Remember that the ending **ary** is more common than **ery**.

A. Complete the following exercises.

1. What ending is added to each word in the word list? _____

2. Although the endings **ary** and **ery** sound very much alike, one ending is far less common than the

   other. That ending is _____ . Write the words from the word list that end in **ary**.

   _____   _____   _____

   _____   _____   _____

   _____   _____   _____

   _____   _____   _____

   _____   _____   _____

   _____   _____   _____

B. On a separate sheet of paper, make a word search puzzle using all 18 spelling words. Trade puzzles with a partner. Try to solve your partner's puzzle. Make a list of all the words you are able to find. How well can you do?

Words ending with *ary*

More Practice

1. temporary	7. complimentary	13. dietary
2. summary	8. extraordinary	14. hereditary
3. literary	9. honorary	15. supplementary
4. secondary	10. voluntary	16. burglary
5. primary	11. contemporary	17. itinerary
6. preliminary	12. solitary	18. necessary

A. Write the words from the spelling list that match the clues and fit the boxes. Circle the hidden word your answers reveal.

1. a name for high schools

2. done by choice

3. before the main event

4. the first in order; basic

5. having to do with books

6. only one

7. lasting only a short time

8. passed through generations

9. having to do with respect

10. existing at the same time

11. a brief report

12. very unusual

13. having to do with food

B. Rearrange the groups of words to make complete sentences. Use correct capitalization and punctuation. Underline the words from the spelling list.

1. necessary be a complete may itinerary not

_____

2. complimentary a received ticket show everyone to the extraordinary

_____

3. the preliminary steps captain took to passengers from burglary safeguard

_____

4. trailer the the used primary as temporary classroom a school

_____

5. vitamins program in this supplementary included are dietary

_____

Lesson 7 Soft and hard *g*

ener**gy**	ea**gle**
re**gi**ster	re**gu**lation
le**ge**nd	le**ga**l
a**ge**nt	ar**gu**ment
ori**gi**n	or**ga**nize
obli**ge**	obli**ga**tion
alle**gi**ance	alli**ga**tor
genius	**gu**itar
re**gi**on	reco**gn**ize

Lesson Generalization: When the letter **g** has a soft sound (**g**inger, **g**ym), it is usually followed by the letter **i, e,** or **y**. When the letter **g** has a hard sound (**g**ame, ma**g**net), it is often followed by a consonant or by the vowel **a, o,** or **u**.

A. Complete the following exercises.

1. Read the words in the word list above. Listen for the soft **g** sound and the hard **g.** What letters follow the soft **g**? _____, _____, _____.

   Write the words from the list that have a soft **g.**

   _____ _____ _____

   _____ _____ _____

   _____ _____ _____

2. What vowels follow the hard **g**? _____, _____, _____.

   Write the words from the word list that have a hard **g** sound.

   _____ _____ _____

   _____ _____ _____

   _____ _____ _____

B. On a separate sheet of paper, write in alphabetical order the nine words that contain a soft **g** sound. Then write in alphabetical order the nine words from the word list that contain a hard **g** sound.

Lesson 7

Soft and hard *g*

More Practice

1. energy	7. allegiance	13. argument
2. register	8. genius	14. organize
3. legend	9. region	15. obligation
4. agent	10. eagle	16. alligator
5. origin	11. regulation	17. guitar
6. oblige	12. legal	18. recognize

A. Use the definitions to find the soft **g** words that fit in the puzzle.

1. loyalty

2. do a favor for

3. a person who acts for another

4. power; force

5. an old story

6. extreme intelligence

7. a beginning

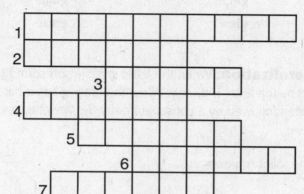

Use the definitions to find the hard **g** words that fit in the puzzle.

1. a rule or law

2. a stringed instrument

3. lawful

4. a large reptile

5. a disagreement

6. to arrange

7. a promise or duty

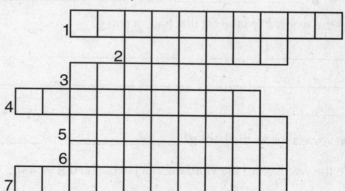

B. Find the misspelled word in each group. Write it correctly on the line.

1. oblige; argument; allegance

_____

2. regaster; alligator; origin

_____

3. genius; reckognize; energy

_____

4. agent; regin; obligation

_____

5. eagel; energy; genius

_____

6. argument; orginize; origin

_____

Review

1. requirement	8. radios	15. construct	21. register
2. separating	9. zeros	16. include	22. legend
3. continues	10. potatoes	17. decision	23. argument
4. introducing	11. revision	18. summary	24. organize
5. performance	12. reelect	19. complimentary	25. energy
6. acquaintance	13. disadvantage	20. voluntary	
7. observance	14. prediction		

A. An analogy is a way of showing how words go together. Look at the first pair of words in each item. How are the words related? Write the spelling word that makes the second pair of words go together in the same way as the first pair.

1. **organize** is to **organizing** as **introduce** is to _____

2. **legend** is to **legendary** as **compliment** is to _____

3. **achieve** is to **achievement** as **require** is to _____

4. **fuel** is to **refuel** as **elect** is to _____

5. **lasso** is to **lassos** as **radio** is to _____

6. **ability** is to **disability** as **advantage** is to _____

7. **assist** is to **assistance** as **acquaint** is to _____

8. **provide** is to **providing** as **separate** is to _____

9. **endure** is to **endurance** as **observe** is to _____

10. **imagine** is to **imagines** as **continue** is to _____

B. Three words in each row follow the same spelling pattern. One word does not. Circle the word.

1. alligator	guitar	oblige	obligation
2. ratios	banjos	silos	declines
3. inspire	inflict	insist	itinerary
4. dietary	honorary	disregard	supplementary
5. consisting	appearing	constructing	providing
6. origin	legal	genius	imagine
7. decision	discourage	disprove	disagreement
8. inspiring	imagining	insisting	completing
9. acceptance	annoyance	inheritance	disadvantage

Review

Lesson 8 **Review**

energy	stereos	zeros
construct	legend	argument
prediction	voluntary	summary
include	revision	decision
allegiance	igloos	alligator
acquaintance	conclude	allowance
disagreement	kangaroo	

A. Complete each phrase with a word from the list.

1. brief _____ of a book

2. six _____ in one million

3. conserve _____

4. the _____ of King Arthur

5. a _____ of the essay

6. music from the _____

7. the weather forecaster's _____

8. an _____ over who waright

9. _____ participation in the project

10. _____ a steel bridge

11. make an important _____

12. will _____ everything on the list

B. Complete each analogy using one of the words from the list.

1. **weak** is to **strong** as **agreement** is to _____

2. **worker** is to **pay** as **child** is to _____

3. **start** is to **begin** as **finish** is to _____

4. **grass** is to **huts** as **snow** is to _____

5. **trunk** is to **elephant** as **pouch** is to _____

6. **help** is to **assistance** as **loyalty** is to _____

7. **tree** is to **monkey** as **river** is to _____

8. **stories** is to **legends** as **numbers** is to _____

9. **sister** is to **relative** as **friend** is to _____

Final *y* words and suffixes

betray ⟶ betrays   betrayed   betraying   attorney ⟶ attorneys

employ ⟶ employs   employed   employing   survey ⟶ surveys

portray ⟶ portrays   portrayed   portraying   ceremony ⟶ ceremonies

qualify ⟶ qualifies   qualified   qualifying   remedy ⟶ remedies

deny ⟶ denies   denied   denying

occupy ⟶ occupies   occupied   occupying

Lesson Generalization: When the letter before a final **y** is a vowel, the **y** does not change when a suffix is added. When the letter before a final **y** is a consonant, change the **y** to **i** before adding **es** or **ed**.

Never change a final **y** to **i** when adding the suffix **ing**.

A. Complete the following exercises.

1. When a suffix is added to a word ending in a vowel-**y** combination, what happens to the **y**?
_____ Write the words from the list that end in a vowel-**y** combination.

_____   _____   _____

_____   _____   _____

_____   _____   _____

_____   _____

2. When a suffix other than **ing** is added to a word ending in a consonant-**y** combination, what happens to the **y**? _____ Write the words from the list that end in a consonant-**y** combination. (Do not include words with the **ing** suffix.)

_____   _____   _____

_____   _____   _____

_____   _____

3. When **ing** is added to any word ending in **y**, what happens to the **y**? _____
_____ Write the words from the list that end in a **y-ing** combination.

_____   _____   _____

_____   _____   _____

B. On a separate sheet of paper, write a short story using at least ten words from the spelling list. Underline the spelling words in each sentence.

Final *y* words and suffixes *More Practice*

1. betrays
2. betrayed
3. betraying
4. employs
5. employed
6. employing
7. portrays
8. portrayed
9. portraying
10. attorneys
11. surveys
12. qualifies
13. qualified
14. qualifying
15. denies
16. denied
17. denying
18. occupies
19. occupied
20. occupying
21. ceremonies
22. remedies

A. Write the base form, the **ed** form, or the **ing** form of a spelling word that completes each sentence.

1. The _____ presented her client's case to the jury.

2. Carolyn could not find a _____ for her cold.

3. Robbie had not _____ to be on the wrestling team.

4. We took a _____ to determine the most popular song.

5. Jennifer received a trophy at the awards _____ held in the gym.

6. Seth _____ a mean character in the school play.

7. The theater will be _____ two more ushers.

8. The movie star had _____ the entire top floor of the hotel.

9. Tom felt that his friend had _____ him by telling the secret.

10. The request for tickets was _____ because it arrived too late.

B. Find and circle 14 words from the spelling list in the word search puzzle. Words appear forward, backward, up, and down.

```
D E Y A R T E B L C Y F Q A T P F
F P N S Z T G Y Y O C C U P I E D
Q T G R E M E D I E S T A G G D H
Z N N B N I D E I N E D L N N G K
L F A G O V B J L X A S I I I Y R
A T T O R N E Y S W V Y F Y Y Q O
M G N I Y A R T R O P O Y O N J F
U O X C Z J L N D K N L I L E G D
R I D S Y E V R U S V P N P D W V
P O R T R A Y S Q X P M G M K L V
B M N C E R E M O N I E S E M V O
G O W D B E T R A Y I N G B O V D
```

Lesson 10

The suffix *able*

tax	+	able	=	tax<u>able</u>	quote	+	able	=	quot<u>able</u>
remark	+	able	=	remark<u>able</u>	value	+	able	=	valu<u>able</u>
comfort	+	able	=	comfort<u>able</u>	imagine	+	able	=	imagin<u>able</u>
respect	+	able	=	respect<u>able</u>	note	+	able	=	not<u>able</u>
consider	+	able	=	consider<u>able</u>	advise	+	able	=	advis<u>able</u>
predict	+	able	=	predict<u>able</u>	rely	+	able	=	reli<u>able</u>
question	+	able	=	question<u>able</u>	vary	+	able	=	vari<u>able</u>
favor	+	able	=	favor<u>able</u>	envy	+	able	=	envi<u>able</u>
bear	+	able	=	bear<u>able</u>
enjoy	+	able	=	enjoy<u>able</u>

Lesson Generalization: The suffix **able**, meaning "able to be," is commonly added to complete words to form adjectives.

taxable = able to be taxed   **imaginable** = able to be imagined

If the base word ends with a silent **e**, drop the **e** before adding the suffix **able**.

If the base word ends with a consonant + **y**, change the **y** to **i** before adding **able**.

A. Complete the following exercises.

1. When the suffix **able** is added to a base word ending in a consonant or a vowel-**y** combination, do not change the spelling of the base word. Write the words from the word list that follow this spelling rule.

_____   _____   _____

_____   _____   _____

_____   _____   _____

_____

2. When the suffix **able** is added to a base word ending in a silent **e,** drop the **e.** Write the words from the list that follow this rule.

_____   _____   _____

_____   _____

3. When the suffix **able** is added to a base word ending in a consonant-**y** combination, change the **y** to **i.** Write the words from the list that follow this rule.

_____   _____   _____

B. On a separate sheet of paper, write the words from the word list in alphabetical order.

Lesson 10 # The suffix *able*

1. taxable	7. questionable	13. imaginable
2. remarkable	8. favorable	14. notable
3. comfortable	9. bearable	15. advisable
4. respectable	10. enjoyable	16. reliable
5. considerable	11. quotable	17. variable
6. predictable	12. valuable	18. enviable

A. Add the **able** suffix to each base word.

1. predict _____   10. value _____

2. rely _____   11. tax _____

3. comfort _____   12. imagine _____

4. consider _____   13. note _____

5. quote _____   14. respect _____

6. vary _____   15. favor _____

7. remark _____   16. question _____

8. enjoy _____   17. advise _____

9. envy _____   18. bear _____

B. Answer each question with the **able** form of a word from the spelling list. The underlined words give a clue to the word you should use.

1. Must you <u>pay a tax</u> on the items you bought?

_____

2. Did the project take <u>a great deal</u> of time?

_____

3. Is that chair <u>nice to sit in</u>?

_____

4. Could you <u>predict</u> the outcome of the game?

_____

5. Was there <u>some doubt</u> about the field trip?

_____

Lesson 11 · Words ending with *al* + *ly*

accidental	+	ly	=	accidentally	verbal	+	ly	=	verbally
intentional	+	ly	=	intentionally	factual	+	ly	=	factually
occasional	+	ly	=	occasionally	global	+	ly	=	globally
additional	+	ly	=	additionally	physical	+	ly	=	physically
incidental	+	ly	=	incidentally	practical	+	ly	=	practically
national	+	ly	=	nationally	typical	+	ly	=	typically
exceptional	+	ly	=	exceptionally	oral	+	ly	=	orally
general	+	ly	=	generally	partial	+	ly	=	partially
usual	+	ly	=	usually	vocal	+	ly	=	vocally

Lesson Generalization: Add the suffix **ly** directly to adjectives ending with **al**. Do not drop the **l** at the end of the base word. Do not drop the **l** in the **ly** suffix.

A. Complete the following exercises.

1. The words in the first column are all what part of speech? _____

2. What part of speech are the words in the second column? _____

3. When you form an adverb by adding **ly** to an adjective ending in **al**, do not drop any letters. Write the adverbs from the word list.

_____   _____   _____

_____   _____   _____

_____   _____   _____

_____   _____   _____

_____   _____   _____

_____

B. Using a dictionary or thesaurus, find synonyms that are also adverbs for each word in the spelling list.

_____   _____   _____

_____   _____   _____

_____   _____   _____

_____   _____   _____

_____   _____   _____

Lesson 11 **Words ending with *al* + *ly***   *More Practice*

1. accidentally
2. intentionally
3. occasionally
4. additionally
5. incidentally
6. nationally

7. exceptionally
8. generally
9. usually
10. verbally
11. factually
12. globally

13. physically
14. practically
15. typically
16. orally
17. partially
18. vocally

A. Write the words from the spelling list that could replace the underlined words.

1. Therese did <u>not</u> drop the dish <u>on purpose</u>.   _____

2. The President is known <u>throughout the nation</u>.   _____

3. <u>In general</u>, the company fills its orders quickly.   _____

4. <u>Sometimes</u> famous people visit here.   _____

5. We are having a <u>characteristically</u> hectic day.   _____

6. Tim expected to present his paper <u>verbally</u>.   _____

7. The company set up offices <u>all over the world</u>.   _____

8. <u>In addition</u>, Leo will need a snorkel and fins.   _____

9. Did Mary put the papers on the table <u>on purpose</u>?   _____

10. Bill spoke <u>with many facts</u> about the issues.   _____

11. Mandy is <u>almost always</u> on time for the games.   _____

12. <u>In physical stature</u>, Allen is larger than Jim.   _____

13. Janet is an <u>unusually</u> good organist.   _____

14. <u>By the way</u>, which book did you decide to buy?   _____

15. The play was <u>almost</u> over when we arrived.   _____

B. Unscramble the letters to make the adjective form of a spelling word.

1. clova   _____

2. lidcctaena   _____

3. realvb   _____

4. neegalr   _____

5. hicaypls   _____

6. rictapcal   _____

7. riltapa   _____

8. tuacfal   _____

The prefix *com*

com + junction = <u>con</u>junction
com + vention = <u>con</u>vention
com + sider = <u>con</u>sider
com + cern = <u>con</u>cern

com + stant = <u>con</u>stant
com + sent = <u>con</u>sent
com + cert = <u>con</u>cert
com + gress = <u>con</u>gress

com + munication = <u>com</u>munication
com + mittee = <u>com</u>mittee
com + mend = <u>com</u>mend
com + mence = <u>com</u>mence
com + mander = <u>com</u>mander

com + bination = <u>com</u>bination
com + plicate = <u>com</u>plicate
com + petition = <u>com</u>petition
com + plaint = <u>com</u>plaint
com + plexion = <u>com</u>plexion

Lesson Generalization: The prefix **com** means "with" or "together." This prefix can be spelled in two ways, **com** or **con,** depending on the root to which the prefix is joined.

It is spelled **com** before roots that begin with the letter **m**, **p**, or **b**. It changes to **con** to make more compatible letter combinations that are easier to pronounce:

Say com**s**tant. Then say con**s**tant.

A. Complete the following exercises.

1. The prefix **com** does not change its spelling when it comes before word roots beginning with

_____, _____ and _____ . Write the

words from the list in which the spelling of **com** remains unchanged when added to a word root.

_____   _____   _____

_____   _____   _____

_____   _____   _____

_____

2. The prefix **com** is spelled **con** before most letters of the alphabet. Write the words from the word list that begin with con.

_____   _____   _____

_____   _____   _____

_____   _____

B. On a separate sheet of paper, write a brief definition of each word in the spelling list.

Lesson 12 The prefix *com*

1. conjunction	7. concert	13. commander
2. convention	8. congress	14. combination
3. consider	9. communication	15. complicate
4. concern	10. committee	16. competition
5. constant	11. commend	17. complaint
6. consent	12. commence	18. complexion

A. Complete each sentence with words from the spelling list. Do not use a word more than once.

1. The band _____ was about to _____
   when the sound system failed.

2. The doctor recommended a special soap to improve my _____.

3. After an hour of _____ pleading, I convinced my father to give his

   _____ .

4. I would never _____ choosing that odd color for my room.

5. Written _____ would be difficult without the help of prepositions and

   _____ .

6. Hundreds attended the annual _____ to express

   _____ about the new policy.

7. The _____ of the army did not hear a single

   _____ from any soldier.

B. Write the words from the spelling list that match the clues.

1. be of interest to	_____	6. rivalry or opposition	_____
2. assembly of government leaders	_____	7. musical performance	_____
3. to praise or honor	_____	8. a union or joining together	_____
4. a word that joins other words	_____	9. a group of appointed people	_____
5. to make difficult	_____	10. a statement of discontent	_____

Lesson 13 Forms of the prefix *ad*

ad	+	vertise	=	advertise	ad	+	opt	=	adopt
ad	+	just	=	adjust	ad	+	ministrator	=	administrator
ad	+	mire	=	admire	ad	+	dressed	=	addressed
ad	+	pear	=	appear	ad	+	pliance	=	appliance
ad	+	ply	=	apply	ad	+	plication	=	application
ad	+	point	=	appoint	ad	+	proximate	=	approximate
ad	+	plause	=	applause	ad	+	pendix	=	appendix
ad	+	prove	=	approve	ad	+	petite	=	appetite
ad	+	proach	=	approach	ad	+	preciate	=	appreciate

Lesson Generalization: The prefix **ad** means "to" or "toward." This prefix can be spelled in different ways. The spelling depends on the root to which the prefix is joined. The prefix **ad** often changes to match the first letter of a root. It changes to **ap** when the root begins with the letter **p**.

Appetite is easier to pronounce than **adp**etite.

Remember why some of these words have double consonants. One of the letters belongs to the root. One belongs to the prefix.

A. Complete the following exercises.

1. The prefix **ad** changes to _____ when it comes before a word root beginning with the letter **p**. Write the examples from the word list that follow this rule.

   _____   _____   _____

   _____   _____   _____

   _____   _____   _____

   _____   _____   _____

2. In most cases, the prefix **ad** does not change when it is added to a word root. Write examples from the word list that follow this rule.

   _____   _____   _____

   _____   _____   _____

B. On a separate sheet of paper, write a short story using at least ten words from the word list.

Lesson 13

Forms of the prefix *ad*

1. advertise
2. adjust
3. admire
4. adopt
5. administrator
6. addressed
7. appear
8. apply
9. appoint
10. applause
11. approve
12. approach
13. appliance
14. application
15. approximate
16. appendix
17. appetite
18. appreciate

A. Write the word from the spelling list that fits in each set of boxes.

1.
2.
3.
4.
5.
6.
7.

8.
9.
10.
11.
12.
13.

B. Circle the misspelled word in each group. Write it correctly.

1. administrator   apply
   adplause   adventure
   _____

2. appreciate   aproach
   adjust   appear
   _____

3. apreciate   approximate
   appendix   appetite
   _____

4. advertise   admire
   apendix   appoint
   _____

Lesson 14

Words ending with *ory*

fac<u>tory</u>	explana<u>tory</u>	direc<u>tory</u>
labora<u>tory</u>	exclama<u>tory</u>	his<u>tory</u>
terri<u>tory</u>	audi<u>tory</u>	satisfac<u>tory</u>
explora<u>tory</u>	introduc<u>tory</u>	prepara<u>tory</u>
vic<u>tory</u>	dormi<u>tory</u>	contradic<u>tory</u>
inven<u>tory</u>	observa<u>tory</u>	deposi<u>tory</u>

Lesson Generalization: The **ory** suffix often follows the letter **t**. The suffix is easy to hear and identify when pronouncing **ory** words of four or more syllables. In **ory** words of three syllables, careless pronunciation can make the suffix difficult to hear.

say <u>his-tor-y</u> not <u>his-try</u>   say <u>vic-tor-y</u> not <u>vic-try</u>

A. Complete the following exercises.

1. Read carefully each word in the word list. Write the words that have only three syllables.

_____   _____   _____

2. The **ory** suffix often follows the letter **t.** When added to words of four or more syllables, the **ory** sound is easy to identify. In three-or-fewer syllable words, careless pronunciation can make the suffix difficult to identify. Write the four-or- more syllable words that have added the **ory** suffix.

_____   _____   _____

_____   _____   _____

_____   _____   _____

_____   _____   _____

_____   _____   _____

B. On a separate sheet of paper, identify each **ory** word as a noun or adjective. Compare your list with a partner's list. Use a dictionary to determine the part of speech for any word on which you do not agree.

Words ending with *ory*

Lesson 14

More Practice

1. factory
2. laboratory
3. territory
4. exploratory
5. victory
6. inventory
7. explanatory
8. exclamatory
9. auditory
10. introductory
11. dormitory
12. observatory
13. directory
14. history
15. satisfactory
16. preparatory
17. contradictory
18. depository

A. Write the word from the spelling list that fits each definition and fits in the boxes.

What additional word do you find hidden in the boxes? _____

1. a record of past events
2. helps you to get ready
3. a large stretch of land; region
4. list of names and addresses
5. place for studying stars, weather
6. place where things are made
7. expressing the opposite
8. acting as an introduction
9. telling how
10. for exploration
11. home for college students
12. listing of items

B. For this exercise, use your dictionary or the results from your work on Exercise B on page 27. Write the ten spelling words that can be nouns. Then write the plural form of each.

Noun	Plural		Noun	Plural
1. _____	_____	6.	_____	_____
2. _____	_____	7.	_____	_____
3. _____	_____	8.	_____	_____
4. _____	_____	9.	_____	_____
5. _____	_____	10.	_____	_____

Lesson 15

Unstressed syllables

sev<u>e</u>ral	prob<u>a</u>bly	comf<u>o</u>rtable
privil<u>e</u>ge	soph<u>o</u>more	rest<u>au</u>rant
diff<u>e</u>rent	pos<u>i</u>tive	temp<u>e</u>rature
gen<u>e</u>rous	int<u>e</u>rest	lit<u>e</u>rature
dec<u>i</u>mal	mem<u>o</u>ry	veget<u>a</u>ble
choc<u>o</u>late	caf<u>e</u>teria	math<u>e</u>matics

Lesson Generalization: The spelling problem in these words is caused by the pronunciation of the words. Some unaccented middle syllables are dropped when the words are spoken. Sometimes the unaccented syllable is easier to hear in another form of the word.

memory: mem<u>o</u>rial   probably: prob<u>a</u>bility

A. Complete the following exercises.

1. Carefully pronounce each word in the word list. Note the underlined letter in each word. These are the letters most frequently left out when one pronounces or spells the

   words. Are these letters consonants or vowels? _____

2. Again, pronounce and then write each word from the word list. As you do, pay close attention to the unaccented (the underlined) vowel in each.

   _____ _____ _____

   _____ _____ _____

   _____ _____ _____

   _____ _____ _____

   _____ _____ _____

   _____ _____ _____

B. On a separate sheet of paper, write each word from the word list. Then write another form of as many words as you can. Compare your list to a partner's.

Lesson 15

Unstressed syllables

More Practice

Tested List

1. several
2. privilege
3. different
4. generous
5. decimal
6. chocolate
7. probably
8. sophomore
9. positive
10. interest
11. memory
12. cafeteria
13. comfortable
14. restaurant
15. temperature
16. literature
17. vegetable
18. mathematics

A. Complete the crossword puzzle with words from the list of spelling words.

Across

2. formal eating place
4. study of numbers
10. informal eating area
11. willing to give
12. recall of the past
13. punctuation to show place in numbers

Down

1. a body of writing
3. unusual
5. year between freshman and junior
6. candy made with cocoa
7. likely to occur
8. many

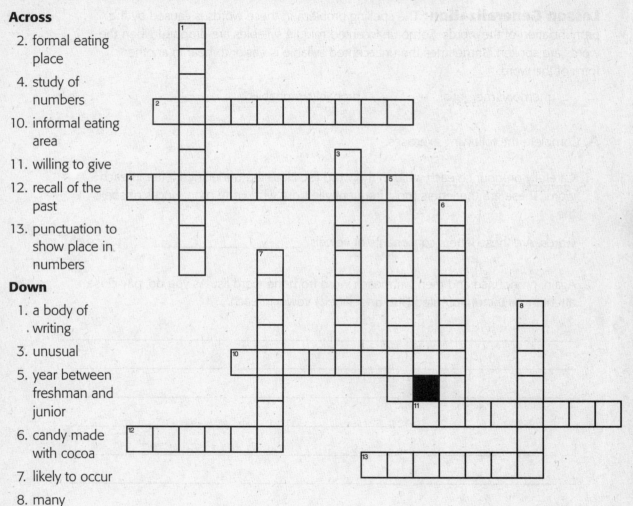

B. Write the word from the spelling list that fits each group of words.

1. curious, concern, regard, _____
2. many, none, few, _____
3. strawberry, vanilla, cherry, _____
4. cozy, easy, snug, _____
5. sure, confident, certain, _____
6. Celsius, Fahrenheit, _____
7. squash, tomato, corn, _____
8. period, dash, comma, _____

Review

Lesson 16

1. employs
2. qualified
3. occupying
4. comfortable
5. valuable
6. reliable
7. usually
8. physically
9. practically
10. nationally
11. consider
12. competition
13. communication
14. combination
15. applause
16. advertise
17. appetite
18. directory
19. history
20. satisfactory
21. several
22. different
23. chocolate
24. temperature
25. probably

A. Complete each analogy with the correct form of a word from the spelling list.

1. **consider** is to **considerable** as **comfort** is to _____

2. **betray** is to **betraying** as **employ** is to _____

3. **combine** is to **combination** as **communicate** is to _____

4. **preparation** is to **preparatory** as **satisfaction** is to _____

5. **general** is to **generally** as **usual** is to _____

6. **deny** is to **denied** as **occupy** is to _____

7. **invent** is to **inventory** as **direct** is to _____

8. **typical** is to **typically** as **practical** is to _____

9. **occupy** is to **occupies** as **qualify** is to _____

10. **vary** is to **variable** as **rely** is to _____

B. Complete each phrase with a word from the list.

competition   valuable   appetite   temperature
reliable   combination   several   physically
advertise   different   chocolate   consider

1. a hearty _____

2. knew _____ of the performers

3. _____ strenuous exercise

4. _____ silver coins

5. the _____ to my lock

6. many _____ types of candy

7. hottest _____ this month

8. a _____ ice cream soda

9. _____ between two teams

10. will _____ your request

11. _____ the product on TV

12. a _____ bus schedule

Name _____ Date _____

Lesson 16 **Review**   *Review*

A. Three words in each row follow the same spelling pattern. One word does not.
Circle that word.

1. observatory	memory	preparatory	exploratory
2. notable	taxable	respectable	considerable
3. complicate	combination	commend	consent
4. portrayed	occupied	employed	betrayed
5. commend	commence	communication	convention
6. factories	remedies	surveys	ceremonies
7. appear	apply	approve	admire
8. factually	occasionally	probably	accidentally
9. predictable	questionable	favorable	valuable
10. several	different	interest	appendix

B. Complete each analogy using a word from the list.

remedy	approximate	restaurant	verbally	commence
valuable	complicated	chocolate	denied	vacuum

1. **thinking** is to **mentally** as **speaking** is to _____

2. **finish** is to **end** as **begin** is to _____

3. **easy** is to **simple** as **difficult** is to _____

4. **praise** is to **flattery** as **cure** is to _____

5. **approved** is to **consented** as **refused** is to _____

6. **deliberate** is to **accidentally** as **worthless** is to _____

7. **student** is to **sophomore** as **flavor** is to _____

8. **beds** is to **dormitory** as **food** is to _____

9. **window** is to **wash** as **carpet** is to _____

10. **exact** is to **specific** as **almost** is to _____

Copyright © McDougal Littell Inc.

Lesson 17 *VAC* words

refer	→ referred	referring	refers
prefer	→ preferred	preferring	prefers
occur	→ occurrence	occurring	occurs
commit	→ committed	committing	commits
forbid	→ forbidden	forbidding	forbids
confer	→ conferred	conferring	confers
rebel	→ rebellion	rebelling	rebels
transfer	→ transferred	transferring	transfers

Lesson Generalization: A **VAC** word has a single **v**owel before a single **c**onsonant in an **a**ccented final syllable. Double the final consonant of a **VAC** word before adding a suffix that begins with a vowel. Do not double the final consonant before adding a suffix that begins with a consonant.

> **v**owel   **c**onsonant   re **fer'**   **a**ccented syllable

A. Complete the following exercises.

1. Circle the correct word or phrase in the following statement.
   (Double/Do not double) the final consonant of a **VAC** word before a suffix
   beginning with a vowel.
   Write the words from the list that end in a suffix beginning with a vowel.

   _____ _____ _____ _____

   _____ _____ _____ _____

   _____ _____ _____ _____

   _____ _____ _____ _____

2. Circle the correct word of phrase in the following statement.
   (Double/Do not double) the final consonant of a **VAC** word before a suffix
   beginning with a consonant.
   Write the words from the list that follow this rule.

   _____ _____ _____ _____

   _____ _____ _____ _____

B. On a separate sheet of paper, write eight sets of original sentences. For each verb
in the first column of the spelling list, write three sentences, one with each form of the
verb listed in the second, third, and forth columns of the spelling list.

Name _____ Date _____

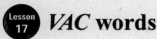

Lesson 17 *VAC* words   *More Practice*

referred	referring	refers
preferred	preferring	prefers
occurrence	occurring	occurs
committed	committing	commits
forbidden	forbidding	forbids
conferred	conferring	confers
rebellion	rebelling	rebels
transferred	transferring	transfers

A. Add the suffix in parentheses to the underlined word and write it on the line.

1. A mistake <u>occur</u> in your spelling. (**s**)_____

2. Are you <u>forbid</u> from wearing jeans to class? (**en**) _____

3. Have you <u>refer</u> to your dictionary to find the meaning? (**ed**) _____

4. Jan <u>prefer</u> the book to the movie. (**s**)_____

5. You <u>confer</u> with the coach. (**ed**) _____

6. Unfair taxes caused the colonists' <u>rebel</u>. (**ion**)_____

7. The suspect <u>commit</u> the crime. (**ed**) _____

8. Tim <u>transfer</u> to a new school. (**ed**) _____

B. Circle the eight words from the spelling list in the word search puzzle. Words are horizontally foward and backward.

F	U	D	E	R	R	E	F	E	R	K	C
G	N	I	R	R	E	F	S	N	A	R	T
P	R	E	F	E	R	R	I	N	G	N	O
R	G	N	I	D	D	I	B	R	O	F	S
E	S	R	E	F	N	O	C	C	U	R	S
D	E	T	T	I	M	M	O	C	T	R	R
U	N	N	O	I	L	L	E	B	E	R	L

Non-*VAC* words

Teaching

travel → traveled	traveling	travels
label → labeled	labeling	labels
model → modeled	modeling	models
cancel → canceled	canceling	cancels
panel → paneled	paneling	panels
edit → editor	editing	edits
credit → credited	crediting	credits
profit → profitable	profiting	profits

Lesson Generalization: Some base words that end in a single vowel before a single consonant do not have a final accented syllable. Do not double the final consonant before adding a suffix to these words.

A. Complete the following exercises.

1. If a word ends in a single vowel before a single consonant, but the final syllable is not accented, what happens to the final consonant when a suffix is added? _____

2. Write the non-**VAC** words from the list that have an added suffix.

_____ _____ _____
_____ _____ _____
_____ _____ _____
_____ _____ _____
_____ _____ _____
_____ _____ _____
_____ _____ _____

B. On a separate sheet of paper, alphabetize all words from the list that have a suffix ending.

Name _____ Date _____

 Lesson 18 # Non-*VAC* words

More Practice

1. traveled	7. modeled	13. paneled	19. credited
2. traveling	8. modeling	14. paneling	20. crediting
3. travels	9. models	15. panels	21. credits
4. labeled	10. canceled	16. editor	22. profitable
5. labeling	11. canceling	17. editing	23. profiting
6. labels	12. cancels	18. edits	24. profits

A. Complete each sentence with two different forms of a spelling word.

1. Juanita takes a course in _____ so she can work with fashion _____.

2. Our garage sale was so _____ that we split the _____ three ways.

3. I am used to _____ by car since I have _____ from Maine to Oregon.

4. The _____ of the magazine may suggest further _____ of your story.

5. Did you have _____ the package, or was it _____ by the post office?

6. We are _____ our plans if the picnic has been _____ because of rain.

7. The wood _____ in the office needs to be _____ again.

8. The past _____ to your account have not yet been _____ .

B. Write the spelling words that match the clues and fit in the puzzle. Each word should use the same suffix that is underlined in the clue.

Across

1. cover<u>ed</u> with sheets of wood
3. give<u>s</u> recognition to
5. display<u>s</u> clothes
6. supervis<u>or</u> of a newspaper

Down

1. cap<u>able</u> of making money
2. name tag<u>s</u>
3. call<u>ed</u> off
4. goe<u>s</u> from place to place

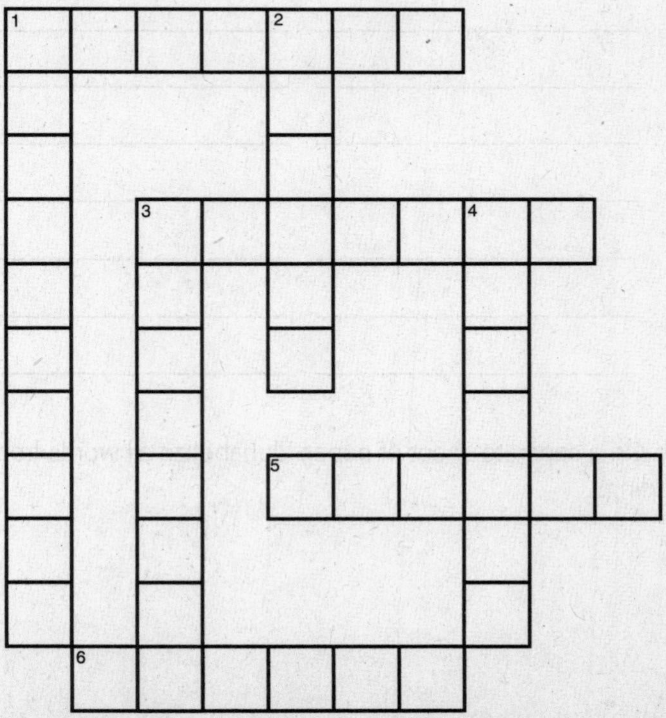

(crossword puzzle grid)

Lesson 19 Words ending with *c* + *ally*

realistic	+ ally	= realist**ically**	rhythmic	+ ally	= rhythm**ically**
historic	+ ally	= histor**ically**	magic	+ ally	= mag**ically**
athletic	+ ally	= athlet**ically**	comic	+ ally	= com**ically**
logic	+ ally	= log**ically**	music	+ ally	= mus**ically**
electric	+ ally	= electr**ically**	mechanic	+ ally	= mechan**ically**
patriotic	+ ally	= patriot**ically**	artistic	+ ally	= artist**ically**
critic	+ ally	= crit**ically**	tropic	+ ally	= trop**ically**
apologetic	+ ally	= apologet**ically**	sarcastic	+ ally	= sarcast**ically**
basic	+ ally	= bas**ically**	tragic	+ ally	= trag**ically**

Lesson Generalization: Words that end with the letter **c** use the ending **ally**. Do not add **ly** directly to the letter **c**.

A. Complete the following exercises.

1. Nouns and adjectives that end in **ic** can be made into adjectives and adverbs by adding the suffix

   _____ .

2. Write the words from the word list that end in **ically**.

   _____ _____ _____

   _____ _____ _____

   _____ _____ _____

   _____ _____ _____

   _____ _____ _____

   _____ _____ _____

B. On a separate sheet of paper, use each word from the spelling list in an original sentence.

Words ending with *c + ally*

More Practice

1. realistically   7. critically   13. musically
2. historically   8. apologetically   14. mechanically
3. athletically   9. basically   15. artistically
4. logically   10. rhythmically   16. tropically
5. electrically   11. magically   17. sarcastically
6. patriotically   12. comically   18. tragically

A. Make a spelling word from the scrambled syllables in each group.

1. cal i crit ly   _____   10. tor ly i his cal   _____
2. cal ot pa i ly tri   _____   11. al re ti is ly cal   _____
3. chan ly i me cal   _____   12. ly i trag cal   _____
4. tri ly lec e cal   _____   13. cal ly mag i   _____
5. cal pol i get o a ly _____   14. cal com i ly   _____
6. ti ly ar tis cal   _____   15. si cal ba ly   _____
7. si cal ly mu   _____   16. ti cas ly sar cal   _____
8. let ly cal i ath   _____   17. cal i ly trop   _____
9. cal rhyth ly mi   _____   18. ly cal log i   _____

B. Write the word that matches each clue.

1. mainly   _____
2. automatically   _____
3. having to do with art   _____
4. in a way that shows love of country _____
5. having to do with criticism   _____
6. in a mocking way   _____
7. dealing with electricity   _____
8. seeing things as they are   _____
9. in a way that shows you are sorry   _____
10. dealing with rhythm   _____

The prefix *ex*

Teaching

ex + tract	= <u>ex</u>tract	
ex + tra	= <u>ex</u>tra	
ex + treme	= <u>ex</u>treme	
ex + tent	= <u>ex</u>tent	
ex + terior	= <u>ex</u>terior	
ex + ternal	= <u>ex</u>ternal	
ex + tinguish	= <u>ex</u>tinguish	
ex + terminate	= <u>ex</u>terminate	
ex + travagant	= <u>ex</u>travagant	

ex + pect	= <u>ex</u>pect	
ex + pense	= <u>ex</u>pense	
ex + periment	= <u>ex</u>periment	
ex + perience	= <u>ex</u>perience	
ex + piration	= <u>ex</u>piration	
ex + pert	= <u>ex</u>pert	
ex + pedition	= <u>ex</u>pedition	
ex + pression	= <u>ex</u>pression	
ex + plode	= <u>ex</u>plode	

Lesson Generalization: The prefix **ex** means "out" or "beyond." It is added directly to roots beginning with the letters **t** or **p**. The letter **x** is never doubled. No commonly used words begin with the letters **exs**. The letter **x** itself makes the sound of **s** or **z**.

A. Complete the following exercises.

1. Add the **ex** prefix directly to roots beginning with the letters _____ and _____. Never double the letter **x**.

2. Write the words from the spelling list in which the prefix **ex** is followed by **t**.

   _____ _____ _____

   _____ _____ _____

   _____ _____ _____

3. Write the words from the list in which the prefix **ex** is followed by **p**.

   _____ _____ _____

   _____ _____ _____

   _____ _____ _____

B. On a separate sheet of paper, write a story of the "exes." Use as many words from the spelling list as you can, and use your imagination.

The prefix *ex*

1. extract
2. extra
3. extreme
4. extent
5. exterior
6. external

7. extinguish
8. exterminate
9. extravagant
10. expect
11. expense
12. experiment

13. experience
14. expiration
15. expert
16. expedition
17. expression
18. explode

A. Complete the sentences with words from the spelling list. Three list words are used in each sentence. No word is used more than once.

1. The _____ of painting the _____ of the old house would

   be costly and foolishly _____ .

2. The _____ from the oil company described the _____ his

   company was conducting to _____ oil from beneath the sea.

3. The _____ of the _____ damage was slight, but the inside

   of the building was nearly destroyed before the firemen could _____ the flames.

4. The _____ cold required the members of the arctic _____

   to wear _____ layers of clothing.

5. Judging by the _____ on his face, he did not consider it a pleasant

   _____ to _____ the rodents.

6. Does the grocer _____ the cans of food to _____ when

   they are kept past their _____ date?

B. First, write the only spelling word that fits in the shaded boxes. Then write ten more words to fit in the boxes across. Use the first word as a clue to the others.

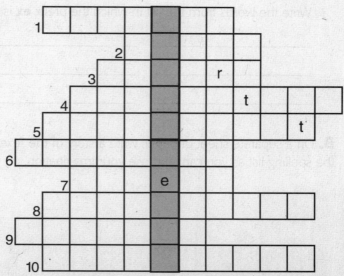

Lesson 21

More forms of the prefix *ad*

Teaching

ad	+	tack	=	<u>att</u>ack		ad	+	cuse	=	<u>acc</u>use
ad	+	tend	=	<u>att</u>end		ad	+	curate	=	<u>acc</u>urate
ad	+	tempt	=	<u>att</u>empt		ad	+	commodate	=	<u>acc</u>ommodate
ad	+	tract	=	<u>att</u>ract		ad	+	company	=	<u>acc</u>ompany
ad	+	tach	=	<u>att</u>ach		ad	+	cumulate	=	<u>acc</u>umulate
ad	+	tention	=	<u>att</u>ention		ad	+	celerate	=	<u>acc</u>elerate
ad	+	titude	=	<u>att</u>itude		ad	+	cented	=	<u>acc</u>ented
ad	+	quaint	=	<u>acq</u>uaint		ad	+	customed	=	<u>acc</u>ustomed
ad	+	quire	=	<u>acq</u>uire		ad	+	complished	=	<u>acc</u>omplished

Lesson Generalization: The adaptable **ad** changes before the letters **t, c,** and **q.** The prefix **ad** becomes **at** before roots that begin with the letter **t.** It becomes **ac** before roots that begin with a **c** or a **q.** Remember why some of these words have double consonants. One of the letters belongs to the root. One belongs to the prefix.

A. Complete the following exercises.

1. The prefix **ad** becomes _____ before roots that begin with the letter **t.** Write the words from the spelling list that follow this rule.

_____   _____   _____

_____   _____   _____

_____

2. The prefix **ad** becomes _____ before roots that begin with the letter **q** or **c.** Write the words from the spelling list that follow this rule.

_____   _____   _____

_____   _____   _____

_____   _____   _____

_____   _____

B. On a separate sheet of paper, make a word search using all of the words from the spelling list. Trade puzzles with a partner and solve your partner's word search.

Lesson 21 # More forms of the prefix *ad*

More Practice

1. attack	7. attitude	13. accelerate
2. attend	8. accuse	14. accented
3. attempt	9. accurate	15. accustomed
4. attract	10. accommodate	16. accomplished
5. attach	11. accompany	17. acquaint
6. attention	12. accumulate	18. acquire

A. Unscramble the syllables to make spelling words. Some groups contain one or two extra syllables.

1. tempt cent ad at _____

2. ti at ten tude _____

3. at ding ad tach _____

4. cum late u ac _____

5. ten tion ac quaint _____

6. ad cur ate ac _____

7. tion at ti ten _____

8. ac mo com date _____

9. com ad ac plished _____

10. ate er cel ac _____

11. tract cur at ti _____

12. late cuse ac com _____

13. cel ac ton quire _____

14. tend trac at ad _____

15. com y ac pan _____

16. tomed cus ion ac _____

17. at ed cent ac _____

18. ad tack at mire _____

B. Write the spelling word that is the synonym (S) or antonym (A) for each word below.

1. discard (A) _____

2. try (S) _____

3. introduce (S) _____

4. blame (S) _____

5. hurry (S) _____

6. repel (A) _____

7. stressed (S) _____

8. adjust (S) _____

9. indifference (A) _____

10. opinion (S) _____

11. give (A) _____

12. inexact (A) _____

13. escort (S) _____

14. unaccustomed (A) _____

Base word changes

Lesson 22

enter → entrance   four → forty

winter → wintry   curious → curiosity

monster → monstrous   generous → generosity

disaster → disastrous

remember → remembrance   explain → explanation

hunger → hungry   maintain → maintenance

                                    detain → detention

Lesson Generalization: A few common words change the spelling of the base
word in an unusual way when a suffix is added. These unexpected spellings result
from dropped or changed vowels.

disaster → disastrous   hunger → hungry

A. Complete the following exercises.

1. Some base words change form when a suffix is added. When a suffix is added to a word

   from the first group, what happens to the **er**? _____

   Write the **er** words from the list that follow this pattern.

   _____ → _____   _____ → _____

   _____ → _____   _____ → _____

   _____ → _____   _____ → _____

2. When a suffix is added to a word from the second group, what happens to the **ou**?

   _____ Write the words from the list that follow this pattern.

   _____ → _____

   _____ → _____

   _____ → _____

3. When a suffix is added to a word from the third group, how does the **ai** change?

   _____ Write the words from this group.

   _____ → _____

   _____ → _____

   _____ → _____

B. On a separate sheet of paper, write 12 sentences. Use one word pair in each.

Base word changes *More Practice*

1. enter	entrance		7. four	forty
2. winter	wintry		8. curious	curiosity
3. monster	monstrous		9. generous	generosity
4. disaster	disastrous		10. explain	explanation
5. remember	remembrance		11. maintain	maintenance
6. hunger	hungry		12. detain	detention

A. Complete each sentence with a spelling word.

1. Although it was January, the weather did not seem _____ .

2. The bus couldn't go through the tunnel because the _____ was closed.

3. Although we'd never forget our trip, we bought postcards as a _____ .

4. The food sent to the _____ flood victims was immensely helpful.

5. We hired a _____ crew to take care of the building.

6. The police will hold the suspects in a _____ cell overnight.

7. I tried to give the answer, but my _____ was not clear enough.

8. Marie's _____ is appreciated by those she helps.

9. If we can save our allowance, we will have the _____ dollars we need.

10. The severe storm was not as _____ as the following earthquake.

B. Write the spelling words that match the clues and fit in the puzzle.

Across

4. a desire to know
6. cold and icy
8. unselfish
9. recollection
10. place to go in
11. interpretation

Down

1. needing food
2. two twenties
3. horrible
5. upkeep
7. confinement

Lesson 23 — Words ending with *cious*, *cial*, or *cian*

Teaching

suspi<u>cious</u>	finan<u>cial</u>	physi<u>cian</u>
deli<u>cious</u>	artifi<u>cial</u>	politi<u>cian</u>
vi<u>cious</u>	spe<u>cial</u>	magi<u>cian</u>
pre<u>cious</u>	ra<u>cial</u>	musi<u>cian</u>
uncons<u>cious</u>	commer<u>cial</u>	pediatri<u>cian</u>
gra<u>cious</u>	so<u>cial</u>	electri<u>cian</u>

Lesson Generalization: The letters **ci** spell the **/sh/** sound in the syllables **cious, cial,** and **cian.**

suspicious	financial	physician

A. Complete the following exercises.

1. Pronounce all of the words in the word list. What sound does the **ci** make in each word?

_____

2. Write all of the words ending in **cious**.

_____ _____ _____

_____ _____ _____

3. Write the words from the word list that end in **cial**.

_____ _____ _____

_____ _____ _____

4. Write the words that end in **cian**.

_____ _____ _____

_____ _____ _____

B. On a separate sheet of paper, write the words from the spelling list in alphabetical order.

Words ending with *cious*, *cial*, or *cian*

Lesson
23

More Practice

1. suspicious
2. delicious
3. vicious
4. precious
5. unconscious

6. gracious
7. financial
8. artificial
9. special
10. racial

11. commercial
12. social
13. physician
14. politician
15. magician

16. musician
17. pediatrician
18. electrician

A. Write an answer for each question, using one of the words from the spelling list. The underlined words will help you decide which words to choose.

1. Was the room decorated with <u>fake</u> flowers?

_____

2. When did Dad take Joey to the <u>baby doctor</u>?

_____

3. Is Ms. Jones <u>active in politics</u>?

_____

4. Does Tom's father <u>repair electrical equipment</u>?

_____

5. Does Billy <u>play the flute</u> well?

_____

6. Wasn't that <u>advertisement</u> effective?

_____

7. Is gold or silver the more <u>valuable</u> metal?

_____

8. Which person <u>performed the magic tricks</u>?

_____

9. Has the theater gone bankrupt because of problems <u>with money</u>?

_____

10. Should all governments strive for equality <u>among races</u>?

_____

11. Does the chocolate cake <u>taste very good</u>?

_____

12. Should you have a <u>doctor</u> look at your injured leg?

_____

B. On a separate sheet of paper, create a word search using all of the words in the spelling list. Trade papers with a partner and solve each other's puzzle.

Lesson 24 Review

1. referred
2. forbidden
3. occurs
4. conferring
5. canceled
6. credited
7. profitable
8. realistically
9. athletically
10. basically
11. magically
12. extra
13. expect
14. expense
15. attention
16. accumulate
17. acquire
18. forty
19. hungry
20. maintenance
21. curiosity
22. detention
23. delicious
24 special
25. physician

A. Complete each analogy with the correct form of a word from the spelling list.

1. **model** is to **modeling** as **credit** is to _____

2. **prefer** is to **preferred** as **refer** is to _____

3. **explanation** is to **explain** as **detention** is to _____

4. **commit** is to **committing** as **occur** is to _____

5. **magical** is to **magician** as **physical** is to _____

6. **detain** is to **detention** as **maintain** is to _____

7. **winter** is to **wintry** as **hunger** is to _____

8. **comic** is to **comically** as **realistic** is to _____

9. **generous** is to **generosity** as **curious** is to _____

10. **critic** is to **critically** as **basic** is to _____

B. Complete each phrase with a word from the list.

magically	occurrence	forty	conferred
expect	acquire	credit	accumulate
attention	profitable	detention	referring

1. got the crowd's _____

2. a _____ fund-raising event

3. didn't _____ to win

4. owned _____ acres of land

5. used a _____ card

6. _____ made a rabbit disappear

7. _____ a pile of newspapers

8. the _____ of the prisoner

9. hope to _____ more stamps

10. not an everyday _____

11. is _____ her to a good doctor

12. _____ with the committee members

Review

Lesson 24

A. Follow the directions to make related forms of spelling words. Remember spelling rules you've learned.

1. acquire	change **ac** to **re**	and	add **ment**	_____
2. attract	change **at** to **dis**	and	add **ion**	_____
3. accurate	change **te** to **cy**	and	add **in**	_____
4. extinguish	change **ex** to **dis**	and	add **ed**	_____
5. external	change **ex** to **in**	and	add **ly**	_____
6. precious	change **ous** to **ate**	and	add **ap**	_____
7. artificial	change **arti** to **of**	and	add **ly**	_____
8. explanation	take off **ex** and **ation**	and	add **ing**	_____
9. expense	change **ex** to **com**	and	add **ation**	_____
10. unconscious	take off **un**	and	add **ly**	_____

B. Three words in each row follow the same spelling pattern. Circle the word that does not follow the pattern.

1. vicious	disastrous	precious	delicious
2. musician	magician	pediatrician	attention
3. expert	expedition	entrance	experience
4. committing	conferring	rebelling	crediting
5. attitude	accurate	accompany	accent
6. travel	prefer	profit	panel
7. patriotically	rhythmically	mechanically	curiously
8. attempt	accomplished	attract	attack
9. external	racial	commercial	financial
10. credited	edited	occurred	labeled

Lesson 25 **Greek combining forms** *Teaching*

astro + naut = astronaut	dia + gram = diagram
astro + logy = astrology	mono + gram = monogram
eco + logy = ecology	tele + gram = telegram
bio + logy = biology	tele + photo = telephoto
mytho + logy = mythology	photo + graph = photograph
peri + scope = periscope	syn + onym = synonym
peri + meter = perimeter	hom + onym = homonym
thermo + meter = thermometer	aristo + cracy = aristocracy
dia + meter = diameter	demo + cracy = democracy

Lesson Generalization: Greek word parts can be combined in different ways to make English words. They are joined in almost the same way English words are joined to make compound words:

telephoto/photograph   touchdown/downstairs

(combined word parts)   (compound words)

Knowing the meaning of the separate parts will help you to understand the many words made by combining the parts.

A. Complete the following exercises.

1. Read the lists of Greek combining forms. Notice that some parts most often appear at the ends of words and others are found at the beginning. What Greek word part is used at both the beginning and end of a word? _____

2. Write the words that are made by combining Greek word parts.

_____   _____   _____

_____   _____   _____

_____   _____   _____

_____   _____   _____

_____   _____   _____

_____   _____   _____

B. On a separate sheet of paper, write a brief definition for each word from the word list.

Greek combining forms

More Practice

1. astronaut	7. perimeter	13. telephoto
2. astrology	8. thermometer	14. photograph
3. ecology	9. diameter	15. synonym
4. biology	10. diagram	16. homonym
5. mythology	11. monogram	17. aristocracy
6. periscope	12. telegram	18. democracy

A. Complete each sentence with the correct word from the word list.

1. The sailors in the submarine used a _____ to look at the fish.

2. The line through the center of a circle is called the _____ .

3. We learned about frog development in our _____ class.

4. Marta applied a _____ to her sweater.

5. Which _____ first set foot on the moon?

6. He used a _____ lens on the camera to get that shot.

7. The word dangerous is a _____ for the word hazardous.

8. On a Celsius _____ , 0 degrees is freezing.

9. Randi took a _____ of the magnificent waterfall.

10. People who study _____ believe that the planets and stars affect our lives.

11. Mark drew a _____ of his invention.

12. Words that are pronounced the same but spelled differently are called _____ .

13. As pollution increases, people become more concerned with _____ .

14. We sent a _____ to my aunt on her birthday.

15. Isabel used string to help her measure the _____ of the desk.

16. In a _____ , every citizen has a duty to vote.

17. Zeus and Hera are characters in Greek _____ .

18. A government ruled by an elite few is known as an _____ .

B. On a separate sheet of paper, use each Greek word part from this lesson to create a word not in the spelling list. Compare your list to a partner's list.

Compound words and contractions

does + not = doesn't	ninety + nine = ninety-nine
should + have = should've	sister + in + law = sister-in-law
could + have = could've	right + handed = right-handed
she + would = she'd	double + header = double-header
who + will = who'll	three + eighths = three-eighths
where + is = where's	half + hour = half-hour
hitch + hike = hitchhike	over + rated = overrated
touch + down = touchdown	wind + shield = windshield
head + light = headlight	wheel + chair = wheelchair

Lesson Generalization: Words can be joined together in several ways. When an apostrophe is used to show that one or more letters have been omitted, the word is called a **contraction**.

doesn't   where's

When two or more words are simply connected with no changes, the word is called a **compound word.** Words joined by a hyphen are another kind of compound word.

touchdown   ninety-five

A. Complete the following exercises.

1. In a contraction, a missing letter or letters are replaced by an _____ .
   Write the contractions from the word list.

   _____   _____   _____

   _____   _____   _____

2. Some compound words are formed when two words are joined without changes to
   either word. Write the compound words from the list that follow this pattern.

   _____   _____   _____

   _____   _____   _____

3. In some compound words, the words are joined by a _____ .
   Write the words from the word list that follow this pattern.

   _____   _____   _____

   _____   _____   _____

B. On a separate sheet of paper, use at least 12 words from the word list in a short story.

Compound words and contractions

More Practice

1. doesn't	7. hitchhike	13. ninety-nine
2. should've	8. touchdown	14. sister-in-law
3. could've	9. headlight	15. right-handed
4. she'd	10. overrated	16. double-header
5. who'll	11. windshield	17. three-eighths
6. where's	12. wheelchair	18. half-hour

A. Write the spelling word that matches each clue. Include hyphens and apostrophes.

1. used in a hospital _____

2. where is _____

3. action in a football game _____

4. two games on the same day _____

5. who will _____

6. glass in car window _____

7. could have _____

8. she would _____

9. my brother's wife _____

10. should have _____

11. too highly thought of _____

12. 100 − 1 = _____

13. travel by asking for rides _____

14. favors right hand _____

15. three parts of eight _____

B. The parts of your spelling words are mixed in the list below to make nonsense words.
Match the parts correctly and write them on a separate sheet of paper under these
headings: Words with Hyphens; Compound Words; and Contractions.

couldinlaw	shouldrated	touchshield	doeslight
doublenine	sisterdown	windwill	hitchhanded
righthave	ninetyhike	overeighths	threeheader
headwould	wheelis	shenot	whohave
wherehour	halfchair		

Lesson 27 The suffix *ible*

poss<u>ible</u>	ed<u>ible</u>	indel<u>ible</u>
permiss<u>ible</u>	elig<u>ible</u>	incred<u>ible</u>
admiss<u>ible</u>	intellig<u>ible</u>	inflex<u>ible</u>
invis<u>ible</u>	tang<u>ible</u>	terr<u>ible</u>
divis<u>ible</u>	dirig<u>ible</u>	horr<u>ible</u>
leg<u>ible</u>	aud<u>ible</u>	combust<u>ible</u>

Lesson Generalization: The suffix **ible** is more commonly used with roots than with complete words. It often follows the letter **s** or the soft **g** sound.

Remember: the hard sound of **c** or **g** is usually followed by the suffix **able.** The suffix **able** is commonly used with complete words.

A. Complete each of the following exercises.

1. Note that the suffix **ible** more often follows roots than complete words. It often follows the letter **s.** Write examples of this spelling pattern from the word list.

   _____ _____ _____

   _____ _____

2. The suffix ible also follows a soft **g**. Write examples of this spelling pattern from the word list.

   _____ _____ _____

   _____ _____

3. Write the remaining words from the word list that end in **ible.**

   _____ _____ _____

   _____ _____ _____

   _____ _____

B. On a separate sheet of paper, use each word from the spelling list in an original sentence. Underline the spelling words. Share your sentences with a partner.

Lesson 27

The suffix *ible*

More Practice

1. possible	7. eligible	13. indelible
2. permissible	8. intelligible	14. incredible
3. admissible	9. tangible	15. inflexible
4. invisible	10. dirigible	16. terrible
5. divisible	11. edible	17. horrible
6. legible	12. audible	18. combustible

A. Write the missing letters for each spelling word.

1. h ___ r ___ i ___ l ___

2. a ___ m ___ s ___ i ___ l ___

3. i ___ d ___ l ___ b ___ e

4. e ___ i ___ i ___ l ___

5. d ___ v ___ s ___ b ___ e

6. i ___ v ___ s ___ b ___ e

7. t ___ n ___ i ___ l ___

8. c ___ m ___ u ___ t ___ b ___ e

9. p ___ r ___ i ___ s ___ b ___ e

10. t ___ r ___ i ___ l ___

11. e ___ i ___ l ___

12. i ___ f ___ e ___ i ___ l ___

13. i ___ c ___ e ___ i ___ l ___

14. l ___ g ___ b ___ e

B. Circle the eleven spelling words in this word search maze. They are forward, backward, and downward.

I	N	D	E	L	I	B	L	E	K	K	Z
S	D	F	D	I	V	I	S	I	B	L	E
E	L	B	I	X	E	L	F	N	I	N	L
E	L	B	I	S	S	I	M	R	E	P	B
E	L	B	I	G	I	L	L	E	T	N	I
A	D	I	R	I	G	I	B	L	E	M	S
A	D	M	I	S	S	I	B	L	E	T	I
I	N	C	R	E	D	I	B	L	E	F	V
I	N	G	E	L	B	I	S	S	O	P	N
E	L	B	I	T	S	U	B	M	O	C	I

Lesson 28 — Forms of the prefixes *ob* and *sub*

ob	+	struct	=	obstruct	sub	+	stitute	=	substitute
ob	+	ject	=	object	sub	+	marine	=	submarine
ob	+	tain	=	obtain	sub	+	urban	=	suburban
ob	+	serve	=	observe	sub	+	traction	=	subtraction
ob	+	pose	=	oppose	sub	+	pose	=	suppose
ob	+	cupy	=	occupy	sub	+	plies	=	supplies
ob	+	casion	=	occasion	sub	+	cessful	=	successful
ob	+	ficial	=	official	sub	+	ficient	=	sufficient
ob	+	fered	=	offered	sub	+	gestion	=	suggestion

Lesson Generalization: The prefix **ob** means "against" or "in the way of." The prefix **sub** means "under," "below," or "in place of." Each of these prefixes can be spelled in different ways. The spelling depends on the roots to which the prefix is joined.

The letter **b** in the prefixes **ob** and **sub** often changes to blend more easily with the first letter of a root. When it changes to match the letters **p, c, f,** and **g,** the result is a double consonant. Remember that one of the double letters in these spelling words is a **b** in disguise.

oppose   sufficient   suggestion

A. Complete the following exercises.

1. The letter **b** in the prefixes **ob** and **sub** often changes to match the first letter of roots beginning with **p, c, f,** and **g.** Write the words from the spelling list that are examples of this spelling pattern.

   _____   _____   _____

   _____   _____   _____

   _____   _____   _____

   _____

2. Write the words from the list in which the prefixes **ob** and **sub** do not change form when they are joined to the roots.

   _____   _____   _____

   _____   _____   _____

   _____   _____

B. On a separate sheet of paper, create a word search puzzle using at least 12 words from the spelling list. Trade papers with a partner and solve your partner's puzzle.

Lesson 28 Forms of the prefixes *ob* and *sub*

More Practice

1. obstruct	7. occasion	13. subtraction
2. object	8. official	14. suppose
3. obtain	9. offered	15. supplies
4. observe	10. substitute	16. successful
5. oppose	11. submarine	17. sufficient
6. occupy	12. suburban	18. suggestion

A. Unscramble the syllables to make spelling words. There are one or more extra syllables in each group.

1. tri ges tion sug _____
2. rine ev ma sub _____
3. fi tro of cial _____
4. py sti cu oc _____
5. ban sub re ur _____
6. lit ject tri ob _____
7. lit pose reg sup _____
8. sti li tute sub _____
9. cian plies sup ly _____

10. tri pose cial op _____
11. stri struct pre ob _____
12. fi suf ply cient _____
13. tain mis ob cur _____
14. ful mar cess suc _____
15. serve lit ob tab _____
16. ca sion ful oc _____
17. tion fered of _____
18. trac un sub tion _____

B. Rewrite each phrase using a spelling word in place of the underlined words.

1. as much wood as we will need _____
2. celebrate the particular event _____
3. block our view of the contest _____
4. studying under the sea life _____
5. watch the birds building a nest _____
6. on the outskirts of the city of Columbus _____
7. person holding a high office in the bank _____
8. furnishes what is needed _____
9. tak the place of our teacher _____
10. get her passport for the trip _____

Name _____ Date _____

Forms of the prefix *in*

Teaching

in	+	patient	=	impatient		in	+	mature	=	immature
in	+	perfect	=	imperfect		in	+	mortal	=	immortal
in	+	practical	=	impractical		in	+	movable	=	immovable
in	+	personal	=	impersonal		in	+	regular	=	irregular
in	+	pure	=	impure		in	+	responsible	=	irresponsible
in	+	proper	=	improper		in	+	resistible	=	irresistible
in	+	prison	=	imprison		in	+	legal	=	illegal
in	+	print	=	imprint		in	+	legible	=	illegible
in	+	press	=	impress		in	+	literate	=	illiterate

Lesson Generalization: The prefix **in** has two common meanings. It may mean "in or into," or it may mean "not or without." The prefix may be spelled in different ways. The spelling depends on the root to which the prefix is joined.

The prefix **in** is spelled **im** before base words that begin with the letters **m** or **p**. It changes to **ir** before the letter **r**. It changes to **il** before the letter **l**. Remember the double consonants when you spell these words.

impatient   irregular   illegal

A. Complete the following exercises.

1. The prefix **in** is spelled _____ before base words that begin with **m** or **p**. Write the words from the word list that follow this pattern.

_____   _____   _____

_____   _____   _____

_____   _____   _____

_____   _____   _____

2. The prefix **in** is spelled _____ before base words that begin with **r**. Write the words from the list that follow this pattern.

_____   _____   _____

3. The prefix **in** is spelled _____ before base words that begin with **l**. Write the words from the list that follow this pattern.

_____   _____   _____

B. On a separate sheet of paper, write a brief definition for each spelling word.

Lesson 29

Forms of the prefix *in*

1. impatient	7. imprison	13. illegal
2. imperfect	8. imprint	14. illegible
3. impractical	9. impress	15. illiterate
4. impersonal	10. immature	16. irregular
5. impure	11. immortal	17. irresponsible
6. improper	12. immovable	18. irresistible

A. Write the spelling word that mean the opposite of each clue.

1. allowed by law _____

2. useful _____

3. can be moved _____

4. having an education _____

5. usual _____

6. have no effect on _____

7. able to put up with delay _____

8. can be opposed _____

9. fully grown _____

10. won't live forever _____

11. faultless _____

12. set free _____

13. respectable _____

14. easy to read _____

15. private or specific _____

16. showing a sense of duty _____

17. clean _____

18. to remove a mark _____

B. Write the spelling word that matches each clue and fits the puzzle.

Across

3. firmly fixed

7. not fully grown

8. not clean

9. not usual

10. not educated

11. not practical

12. against the law

Down

1. not suitable

2. having a fault or flaw

4. too strong to resist

5. living forever

6. not patient

The suffixes *ence* and *ent*

Teaching

aud<u>ience</u>	interfer<u>ence</u>
obed<u>ience</u>	circumfer<u>ence</u>
viol<u>ence</u>	differ<u>ence</u>
sil<u>ence</u>	coincid<u>ence</u>
abs<u>ence</u>	sci<u>ence</u>
pres<u>ence</u>	
pat<u>ience</u>	presid<u>ent</u>
intelli<u>gence</u>	frequ<u>ent</u>
influ<u>ence</u>	delinqu<u>ent</u>
evid<u>ence</u>	

Lesson Generalization: The suffixes **ence** and **ent** are commonly added to roots. They are often used after the letters **fer** and **qu.**

interference   frequent

A. Complete the following exercises.

1. The suffixes **ence** and **ent** often follow roots ending in the letters _____ or
_____.

2. Write the words from the spelling list that end with the suffix **ence.**

_____   _____   _____

_____   _____   _____

_____   _____   _____

_____   _____   _____

_____   _____   _____

3. List the words that have the suffix **ent.**

_____   _____   _____

B. On a separate sheet of paper, scramble the spelling words. Then trade papers with
a partner and unscramble each other's words. Who can solve all 18 words first?

Lesson 30: The suffixes *ence* and *ent*

1. audience	7. patience	13. difference
2. obedience	8. intelligence	14. coincidence
3. violence	9. influence	15. science
4. silence	10. evidence	16. president
5. absence	11. interference	17. frequent
6. presence	12. circumference	18. delinquent

A. Complete each sentence with a word from the spelling list.

1. I took my dog to _____ school to be trained.

2. Joan had an excused _____ from school.

3. The _____ cheered the remarkable performance.

4. The lawyer presented _____ of the suspect's guilt.

5. It was a _____ that both of us brought the same CDs.

6. Will the politician's campaign _____ the voters?

7. Many people object to the _____ on some TV programs.

8. The crowd watched in complete _____ as the gymnasts performed.

9. The tenant received a notice because he was _____ in paying his rent.

10. Lil's _____ at the meeting was required in order to hold the election.

11. Taking care of very young children requires a great deal of _____ .

12. When Angelo got braces, he made _____ trips to the orthodontist.

13. Don measured the _____ of the ball with a string.

14. The _____ we are getting on our radio is caused by the storm.

15. Because of his great _____ , Einstein was considered a genius.

16. The _____ between six and four is two.

17. Biology is the _____ of plant and animal life.

18. Our club is preparing to elect a new _____ .

B. Each of the following words is contained in one of your spelling words. On a separate sheet of paper, write the word, the spelling word, and a sentence using the spelling word. Do not use any spelling word more than once.

1. flu	3. pat	5. side	7. coin	9. deli
2. tell	4. bed	6. die	8. den	10. if

Name _____ Date _____

Words ending with *ize* or *ise*

Teaching

special	+	ize	=	special<u>ize</u>		modern	+	ize	=	modern<u>ize</u>
central	+	ize	=	central<u>ize</u>		hospital	+	ize	=	hospital<u>ize</u>
visual	+	ize	=	visual<u>ize</u>		character	+	ize	=	character<u>ize</u>
capital	+	ize	=	capital<u>ize</u>		immune	+	ize	=	immun<u>ize</u>
item	+	ize	=	item<u>ize</u>		harmony	+	ize	=	harmon<u>ize</u>
idol	+	ize	=	idol<u>ize</u>		monopoly	+	ize	=	monopol<u>ize</u>

surpr<u>ise</u>   exerc<u>ise</u>

disgu<u>ise</u>   adv<u>ise</u>

telev<u>ise</u>   merchand<u>ise</u>

Lesson Generalization: The suffix **ize** is added to complete words to form verbs meaning "to make or become."

modernize = "to make modern"   centralize = "to make central"

When the suffix is added to complete words, it is usually spelled **ize.**

Notice how a final **e** or **y** are dropped when the suffix is added.

The **ise** spelling is less common. It is usually part of the base word itself rather than a suffix:

surprise   televise

A. Complete the following exercises.

1. The suffix **ize** is usually added to complete words to form verbs meaning "to make or become." Write the words from the list that end in **ize.**

   _____   _____   _____

   _____   _____   _____

   _____   _____   _____

   _____   _____   _____

2. The **ise** ending is more often a part of the word than a suffix. Write the words from the word list that end in **ise.**

   _____   _____   _____

   _____   _____   _____

B. On a separate sheet of paper, write the **ize** and **ise** words in alphabetical order. Check your work with a partner.

Lesson 31 # Words ending with *ize* or *ise*   *More Practice*

1. specialize	7. modernize	13. surprise
2. centralize	8. hospitalize	14. disguise
3. visualize	9. characterize	15. televise
4. capitalize	10. immunize	16. exercise
5. itemize	11. harmonize	17. advise
6. idolize	12. monopolize	18. merchandise

A. Decide whether **ize** or **ise** should be added to each word or letter group. Then write the complete word.

1. disgu _____   10. immune _____

2. central _____   11. surpr _____

3. character _____   12. item _____

4. adv _____   13. monopoly _____

5. merchand _____   14. special _____

6. harmony _____   15. visual _____

7. exerc _____   16. idol _____

8. telev _____   17. modern _____

9. capital _____   18. hospital _____

B. Write the spelling word that matches each clue and fits in the boxes.

1. worship

2. bring up to date

3. give an opinion

4. picture in the mind

5. put in a hospital

6. vigorous movements

7. costume

8. to make a special study

Lesson 32 **Review**

thermometer	official	illegible	audience
astrology	occasion	immature	absence
diagram	suggestion	imperfect	frequent
biology	submarine	capitalize	
should've	invisible	hospitalize	
could've	possible	surprise	
hitchhike	eligible	exercise	
ninety-nine			

A. Complete each analogy with the correct form of a spelling word.

1. **imperfectly** is to **imperfect** as **frequently** is to _____

2. **surprise** is to **surprised** as **capitalize** is to _____

3. **should have** is to **should've** as **could have** is to _____

4. **obtain** is to **object** as **occupy** is to _____

5. **exercise** is to **exercising** as **hitchhike** is to _____

6. **invisible** is to **visible** as **ineligible** is to _____

7. **possible** is to **impossible** as **perfect** is to _____

8. **capital** is to **capitalize** as **hospital** is to _____

9. **legible** is to **illegible** as **mature** is to _____

10. **surprise** is to **surprising** as **exercise** is to _____

B. Complete each phrase with a word from the list.

astrology	biology	thermometer	absence
should've	occasion	surprise	suggestion
audience	eligible	ninety-nine	invisible

1. _____ been more careful

2. an excused _____ from school

3. read 15° on the _____

4. used a microscope in _____

5. loud applause from the _____

6. _____ years old

7. threw a _____ party

8. read an _____ chart in the paper

9. celebrated the special _____

10. _____ without a telescope

11. not _____ for the team

12. made an excellent _____

Lesson 32 **Review**

A. Three words in each row follow the same spelling pattern. One word does not. Circle the word that does not fit.

1. intelligible	possible	immovable	audible
2. disguise	obtain	headlight	surprise
3. silence	immature	suppose	advise
4. incredible	impurity	indelible	invisible
5. should've	she'd	three-eighths	could've
6. object	obtain	observe	oppose
7. performance	circumference	obedience	interference
8. astronaut	periscope	hitchhike	biology
9. half-hour	right-handed	wheelchair	double-header
10. hospitalized	itemized	televised	visualized

B. Complete each analogy with a word from the list.

circumference	exercise	audible	submarine
ninety-nine	silence	infrequent	windshield
diameter	astronaut	oppose	imperfect

1. **seen** is to **visible** as **heard** is to _____

2. **light** is to **dark** as **noise** is to _____

3. **three** is to **nine** as **thirty-three** is to _____

4. **often** is to **frequent** as **seldom** is to _____

5. **air** is to **plane** as **water** is to _____

6. **skill** is to **practice** as **fitness** is to _____

7. **line** is to **length** as **globe** is to _____

8. **ship** is to **sailor** as **rocket** is to _____

9. **around** is to **perimeter** as **through** is to _____

10. **agree** is to **support** as **disagree** is to _____

11. **house** is to **window** as **car** is to _____

12. **flawless** is to **perfect** as **damaged** is to _____